APPRECIATION

Heartfelt thanks go to Laura Lorance and Larry Brethauer who, without their tireless hours of support and encouragement, this work would not have happened. May God richly bless you for your encouragement and help.

Contents

Preface xi
Introduction xiii

Chapter : 1 The Beginning of the End 17
Chapter : 2 Despair to Hope 23
Chapter : 3 Consequences not Removed 27
Chapter : 4 Sin Ushers in Consequences 41
Chapter : 5 Alone, Broken, and Humbled 47
Chapter : 6 Challenged, but Seeing God 53
Chapter : 7 Deliverance Is Sweet 63
Chapter : 8 The Beginning of a New Life 75
Chapter : 9 The Shaping of a New Life 87
Chapter : 10 The Call to Preach 101
Chapter : 11 The Call to Plant 113
Chapter : 12 Moving Us Forward 123
Chapter : 13 Life Lessons 149

PREFACE

It is with great humility and gratefulness that I share my personal testimony. I am certainly not proud of my past, nor do I desire any credit as some self-made man, for I have sufficiently messed up about as good as any person can. Rather, I share my life with you, so my God might receive all the glory for lives that not only have been touched and changed, but are being changed even as I write. So I want to make clear that I share the following with a great desire to see God praised, honored, and glorified. It is my desire that anyone who reads this book will realize there is no such thing as a "lost cause" with Christ.

God is a redeemer of broken lives and can heal yours, even if your past is full of failure. He takes broken lives, heals them, and puts them on a new path—a pathway to His fullness. Also, the Bible says in Revelation 12:11, "They overcame him [Satan] by the blood of the Lamb and by the word of their testimony…" Therefore, by writing this book, I propose to position myself to defeat Satan in my life.

This is my story. I want to invite you into my home, into my living room, to sit down in front of the fire in a comfortable chair and just listen to what my mighty God has done (and is doing) in my life.

—Doyl

INTRODUCTION

> Enter through the narrow gate; for the gate is wide and the way is broad that leads to destruction, and there are many who enter through it.
> —Matthew 7:13

A bitter cold snap hit two days before Thanksgiving, 1980—very unusual for this southern delta state, Louisiana. My wife and I were locking up our clothing store after our normal twelve-hour day when I received a phone call from a friend. Not the kind of friend you'd want to hang out with or trust with anything of value, but just a business friend. The voice on the other end gave our normal greetings, and then, in the code language only we understood, he requested a buy. I signaled to come by my home in about an hour. My wife went to do some shopping while I hurried home to accommodate his need—and to help fund mine.

When I arrived home, I stepped behind the house to a secret hiding place (which most of the time made me feel secure because of an unreasonable idea that no one could ever find it) and picked up a garbage bag. It was a large, lumpy, black bag weighing only about ten pounds. I made my way carefully back to the front of the house, so as not to be seen by anyone. Once in the house, I warmed myself first and then began to separate the bag's contents—a large quantity of marijuana that had been shipped in from Hawaii. This was an incredible stash of the best holiday weed anyone could have landed in the drug world. This high-dollar sack of "get high" weed would bring some $20,000 dollars, depending on how much patience I exercised. Of course, I only wanted a few small bags for my party friends and myself. I was purchasing the large quantities to fund my real need—the holiday party life, which cost thousands of dollars.

My business friend arrived soon and knocked on the door. He came in, sat down, and we talked about his family in one breath and the drugs he was looking for in the next. I proudly brought in the sack of choice marijuana for his selection process. He smelled it and quickly rolled up a joint to try it out. After some time of testing, he was blown away with its quality and agreed to purchase a small quantity. However, something seemed strange about him…he seemed nervous…a little on edge…I asked about it, but he blew it off and then left.

I did not know why, but I had a strange feeling about this deal. I had prided myself on my ability to keep one step ahead of the authorities, and I did not intend for this to change. I carefully bundled up several pounds for a delivery later that evening, while the balance, still a large quantity, I returned to my hiding place. Then I left to make a routine delivery. Everything went according to plan, and when I arrived back home very late, I went to bed.

The next day, Thanksgiving eve, found us so busy at the store that before we knew it, the day was over. This night was even colder, and as we drove home a weather front was moving in with a prediction of freezing rain and sleet. We quickly stopped by a small grocery store to pick up a few items and then went straight home. The next morning, we planned to leave with my mother and travel to Florida for our first-time-ever family reunion.

We were very tired from the holiday rush and settled in to a warm fire and our favorite music. However, I could not get that drug deal out of my mind. It lingered like some bad taste that would not go away. I felt like something was wrong but could not put my finger on why I felt this way.

Out of some weird impulse, I retrieved the sack of marijuana and began to think in a what-if-someone-came-looking-for-drugs thought process. Where would they not look? I looked around outside and noticed our garbage can was sitting out front, ready to roll out to the street the next day. I thought if someone came looking, who would look for drugs in a garbage can in front of our house? I cannot say whether I was all there on this thought process—it's just what I thought! So, I proceeded out of our house with the black garbage bag, pulled the garbage sack out of the trash can, placed the drug one in first, and then followed it with our real garbage. As I put the lid on the garbage can, it began to sleet.

Little did I know that in a few hours, my life was going to make a radical turn—a turn I was not in any way prepared for, nor did I ever think would happen to me. It would be one of those turns that forever changes the landscape of your life and forces you to take stock in yourself—one that forces you to consider who you are, what you are, and begs the question, "Where am I going?"

THE BEGINNING OF THE END

> But if you will not do so, behold, you have sinned against the LORD, and be sure your sin will find you out.
> —Numbers 32:23

I had a very happy childhood, growing up in the mid fifties and sixties in a small town on the northwestern coastline of California. I came from a wonderful family and heard about God at an early age. My mother made sure I attended church regularly—just about every time the door was opened. It was somewhat expected since we lived just one block from our local church. We would all go together on most Sunday mornings as a family, but just Mom and the kids went for the rest of our meeting times.

As I stepped out in life, I had big dreams—dreams of money, social status, business success, and retirement at thirty-five. I was definitely motivated by selfish desires and objectives. God was nowhere in the picture. Oh, I believed God was real; I just did not have any room for Him in my life. I remember traveling between cities one day and telling God to go ahead and run the world—but I would run my own life!

In pursuit of these self-centered dreams, my brother and I partnered to open a clothing business in a small Louisiana town. Actually, it was only a seventies "jean shop" in the beginning, but it developed into a complete men's and ladies' clothing store. This business venture played right into my goals and ego. Overnight (it seemed) I achieved respect, status, and certainly cash flow (but not much real money). And I was on my way. I drove a Corvette and became the talk of the town.

I met my wife, Vonette, in this small town. She, too, had learned about God in Sunday school; however, she had also left all the teachings of Jesus behind and was looking for whatever life had to offer. We hit it off at first sight. I would not call it love at first sight on my part, but more of lust at first sight…Me for her, but for her? My car! Anyway, we began a relationship, and she quickly became involved with my pursuits, desires, and business direction. I added a ladies' section to our store, and she managed it completely. We dated for a couple years and were finally married in August of 1978.

We quickly became very important figures in the social structure of this small town. We were successful, nice looking, and had money. We were great party people, and other people enjoyed our free spirits. Together, we set our sights on opening many more stores to achieve even more money and success. Little did we know we were on a course that would lead to disaster. There was an iceberg in our path, but we just kept going "full steam ahead"!

As we pursued our goals, they began to take a toll on us. We worked very hard in our business. We did everything. We worked some twelve hours a day, six days a week, and then on Sunday trying to catch up balancing our books. This was an impossible pace to maintain, so friends introduced us to some pills that would help us take on the challenge of our fast-paced life. We gladly accepted their suggestion and quickly became even better at accomplishing our goals.

It was not long until we purchased another store, and we thought we were on our way. However, we had a problem. We could not seem to sleep at night because of the pills we were using, so we took another type of pill to help us rest. We also began to use other drugs to support different aspects of our busy lifestyle. Marijuana certainly was one used to enhance our party life. Our drug use evolved slowly, progressing over time.

At this point, I really thought we had it all. We had status, respect, and many of the things important to us. We would travel to the Dallas apparel market to purchase clothing and accessories for our next season's business. We'd spend thousands of dollars with the dealers, and they'd reward us with lines of cocaine in the back rooms and invitations to parties where drugs, alcohol, food, and party people were all provided. We fell right into Satan's trap! We took the bait...hook, line, and sinker.

Within our own minds, we had built a great "cloud of justification" around our actions. We *needed* the drugs. First, we needed them to follow the markets' example by having drugs on hand to share with our best customers (the ones who spent large amounts of money with us). We also needed the drugs to always appear happy and full of energy. Finally, we needed the drugs to function....really, to exist! But understand, we never thought we were doing anything seriously wrong. We were not hurting anyone else. This was our life, and we deserved to choose what we wanted to do. It was our right! In fact, I remember telling my wife that if the authorities wanted to arrest us for a few bags of marijuana...well just let them come. Such arrogance!

Our drug involvement grew to a point that even with all the money we were earning, we just did not have enough to get the drugs we craved—the "best of the best." This required purchasing larger quantities, which required larger sums of money. I began to recruit friends to go in together, so we could all enjoy the best of the drugs. This turned into a way to pay for our drug needs.

Without fully thinking through what I was doing, I turned my need into a drug business. On Thanksgiving eve, 1980, our lives were shattered as all this false world of happiness, success, and security came crashing down on us.

A good friend had stopped by our home, and we played a game of backgammon while snorting lines of cocaine and smoking choice Hawaiian marijuana. Even though I should have been feeling pretty laid back, for some unknown reason I just could not get rid of this uneasy felling in my gut...I felt weird...like my skin was crawling.... Then, there was this total silence. It felt like time had stood still. Even the air did not move.

Quickly, moving by instinct, I gathered up all the drugs in my living room and walked directly to my bathroom. Then, suddenly, narcotics agents broke through our front and back doors, looking for what they thought would be a very large quantity of drugs. I immediately flushed as much as I could before they made it to my bathroom.

Vonette, my friend, and I were forced down on the couch and held at gun point. At this moment, my life flashed before me, almost like some kind of "out of body experience." I could see myself when I was young. My life paraded before me in living color. It was a happy childhood, my parents were very loving, and I possessed a hope for a bright future. What had gone wrong? What was I going to do now? How would I get out of this?

I could see outside through a window, and I was amazed at the large numbers of men involved with this bust. Then I saw what I thought would be the sure nail in my coffin—a drug dog! They were walking him around the house in a complete sweep of the outside premises. Fear gripped me! They were searching near our outside trash can.

Everything moved in slow motion...step by step...closer and closer.... I tried not to stare, afraid I would give it away, but how would they miss it with a dog! The dog got to the trash can and sniffed it. The officer opened the lid, and the dog jumped up to the top and sniffed several times. Then the most amazing thing happened—they put the top back on and continued their search! I could not believe it. The dog did not catch the scent! Somehow, the sleet and garbage combined to throw off the dog's smell. I could not believe it!

At this point, we were shown a search warrant that allowed them to completely search our home. The result of that search yielded two bags of marijuana, five Quaalude pills, and a trace of cocaine. As we sat on the couch reflecting on what was happening, Vonette looked at me and said she felt like God was trying to tell us something, but I responded by blaming God for where we were. I certainly did not want anything to do with Him. We were arrested that night for possession of marijuana with intent to distribute, possession of Quaalude pills, and possession of cocaine. We were taken to the parish jail facility where we immediately posted bond.

It was not long until our world collapsed around us. We began to lose everything. All our so-called friends fled like rabbits to their holes. People would not continue shopping with the "druggies" of the town, and mothers would not allow their children to come and purchase their clothes from us anymore. In what seemed to be one night, but was really the course of years, our lives were crumbling around us. No respect, no status, no friends, nowhere to turn. At this point, we turned from illegal drugs to the legal drug of alcohol. We began to drink heavily, bottle after bottle, trying to numb the circumstances we faced—a possible fifteen years in prison!

Chapter 2

DESPAIR TO HOPE

Therefore, if any man be in Christ, he is a new creature: old things are passed away; behold, all things are become new.
—2 Cor 5:17 (KJV)

Over a period of six months, we lost everything. Our business failed, we could not pay our bank notes or creditors, and we were considering bankruptcy. Time would produce some seven judgments filed against us, totaling over fifty-thousand dollars. It seemed like everybody and their brother wanted something out of me. I could not find work anywhere in town and had no place to run. Eventually my father-in-law, who ran an upholstery shop, agreed to give me a job. I went from ten-thousand dollars a week to about one-hundred dollars a week.

I was severely depressed and did not know what to do. Vonette and I were merely trying to survive. Too distressed by our own fears and desperation to help each other, we just existed. Should we try to escape to another country, like to Canada? Should we leave everything and everyone we knew, just to be free?

The thoughts she had voiced on the couch the night of our arrest, about God getting our attention, kept surfacing with the idea that we should attend church. "Not me!" I would spew out. "Look what He (God) has done to us now. I will not have anything to do with Him!" It is hard to imagine how deep my despair was. The only occasional bright spot was the support of our parents (Vonette's mom and dad, Jeanette and Vonnie, and my mother, Dorothy). Their love and support was invaluable and flowed like a river in spite of our failure.

After our arrest some four months later, Vonette's cousin came by to offer support. He shared that God was the answer to our problems, and if she ever needed a ride to church, to give him a call. He would be glad to pick her up. Well, this idea needed time to develop. It's not that it wasn't the right answer; it just needed to soak into a confused mind. On a Wednesday night in April of 1981 some six months after our arrest, Vonette told me she was going with her cousin to church—to a prayer meeting.

Of course, I did not need a prayer meeting. That night, I fixed my normal high-balls. First, second, but by the third high-ball, the typical numbing did not come. I was sitting in a rocking chair in my living room. The TV was on, but I could not really hear it. There was a heaviness in the room…a coldness sweeping across my body…. The wall seemed to applaud with my despair, like some huge stadium of fans cheering me on to the deepest despair. Thoughts came piercing into my being.

You are a loser! the first thought screamed. I found myself agreeing. *I am a loser,* I thought. Why not? Everything I had valued was now gone.

You are worthless, came the second, more destructive thought, pointing to the way I was already feeling about myself. I had not only ruined my life, but my dear wife Vonette's as well. I had led her down this path, destroying all hope of either of us being successful. Again, I found myself agreeing.

It is hopeless. The third thought added more support to my total failure. Who would want to hire someone like me? How would

I find a career or make a quality livelihood? My life was hopeless, and there was no future for me.

Finally, the goal of all of these thoughts came together to lead to the final blow. The crowds in the stands seem to cheer even louder. The cult-like chant, *Do it!...Do it!...Do it!...* began to rise and swell. Satan then placed the final blow with, *Life is not worth living!*

At this moment, a cold chill raced across my body, and a sweat broke out at the same time. I was on the verge of rising from the chair, walking to my back bedroom where I kept my gun, putting it to my head, and ending my worthless life—I was ready to take my own life! I had reached the very bottom...broken.

By now the chant, *Do it!...Do it!...Do it!...* had reached a level so that I could hear nothing else. At a fever pitch, the demons were screaming out, *Do it!...Do it!...Do it!....* Their voices rang with confidence because they had done this successfully so many times before. They moved in on me like tigers for the kill.

In that moment, a very small part of me remembered my mother taking me to church, remembered there *was* a God, remembered a Jesus who had given His life for me—and I could turn to Him! In this split second a shaft of light pierced the coldness and heaviness in my living room. It dispelled the chanting crowds and applauding walls and the hopelessness in my heart. It brought warmth, life, acceptance, forgiveness.

I fell out of the rocking chair and on to my knees and face, and cried out, "Oh God, I need You! I don't know what to say. I don't know what to do. I don't know how to act. All I know is that I need You, and I need You now!" As I looked up, I saw Jesus! I wept because of my unworthiness in the presence of our Lord Jesus Christ.

He was standing there in a bright white robe with His arms extended out toward me as if to say, *"Come unto Me, I love you."* His presence radiated light, warmth, love, forgiveness, and acceptance. He had dispelled all hopelessness and despair and instead ushered in salvation, hope, and a future—a new beginning I could not even dream of! In April of 1981, I became a new man in Christ! He threw me a lifeline and asked me to hold on tight. I had a long way to go…

My wife returned home to a new man—a man who had given his life to Jesus Christ as Lord and Savior. I became a man with new vision, new dreams, and new hopes that night. God Almighty became real in a way I had never experienced before. What I must face with my arrest had not gone away, but the way I would handle it would be very different.

As amazing as this conversion was, I was just as surprised when I learned that at the very moment I was warring in the spiritual realm, believers at my wife's prayer meeting were calling out our names before the Lord! They were pleading with Him to work in our lives, praying for me to turn to Him. The concert of love our God orchestrates is a movement too wonderful for words.

Chapter 3

CONSEQUENCES NOT REMOVED

Then David said to Nathan, "I have sinned against the LORD." And Nathan said to David, "The LORD also has taken away your sin; you shall not die.

—2 Samuel 12:13

With this new-found Savior came a new hope. But I found myself not knowing what to do, so we began attending the local church, hoping to find direction and answers. I will never forget our first visit to this church. I cannot remember the service itself, but I really remember the pastor's invitation.

Vonette and I were sitting on a pew near the back of an approximately 400-seat worship center. The pastor was calling people to be real with the Lord. He asked the congregation to not be ashamed of Him, but to come to the front and proclaim Jesus as Lord of their lives.

They started singing a song, "Just as I am, without one plea…" As they were singing, my heart began to pound. I mean, it was beating so hard I thought it would come out of my chest. As I stood there, I grasped the pew in front of me and held on tightly—so tightly, my knuckles turned white.

In one ear, I heard a voice saying, "Go and proclaim that you belong to Me, tell the people you are Mine." In the other ear, immediately following this, I heard another message, "Don't go down there. They will laugh at you and make fun of you." Then back in the other ear, "Go and tell them you mean business with Me." Then again, in the other ear, "They will not believe you. They will think you are doing this because you are in trouble and just want to look good for the court system." Once again, in the other ear, "Go My child, I want you to go." Without question, a war was being waged for my soul, back and forth, back and forth. My heart desired to know God, but my flesh was unsure what to do.

I ached deep inside, wanting to obey God, but so ashamed of my past. Wanting to go God's way, but feeling like others would laugh. Even my bones seemed to cry out in distress. It felt like an eternity. They sang one verse…then the chorus…then the next verse…then the chorus….

At this point, I thought the pastor was going to end it. He stepped up to the microphone and surprised me completely. He did not end it, but he again asked us not to delay, not to say no to the Savior, but to come and let Him have His way with our lives. These words were like streams of fire burning deep into my soul, igniting a flame. A flame that burned more and more brightly, until I thought, *I don't care what others think. I don't care about my past. I don't care if I don't have all the answers. I just want to know and follow Him.*

Realizing that my heart was fixed on pleasing God, I turned to walk toward the aisle. As I took my first step, I felt Vonette's hand slipping into my arm. I turned to see what she wanted. Our eyes met. Her eyes said it all. She too was ready to tell everyone that we believed in Jesus Christ, and we were ready to follow Him wherever He would lead our lives.

Our first few steps toward the aisle were so difficult. I felt as though I was carrying a thousand-pound weight on my back. I was hardly able to take a step. My legs trembled, and I wondered if I might fall, but we finally reached the aisle.

I took in a breath. It looked like it was a mile long. There seemed to be thousands of people laughing and pointing at us in that moment. I stood there for what seemed like an hour, fighting off the perceived laughter. As we made the first, second, and third steps, the weight became lighter and lighter.

My eyes locked with the pastor's, and then an amazing thing happened. The laughter was replaced by thousands of voices praising and glorifying God. By the time we reached the front of the church, the weight was gone. It had turned into the great and wonderful joy of the Lord.

I wept much as I tried to communicate to the pastor our desire to follow Christ. He was so full of love and acceptance. He patiently allowed me to share our desires with him, and he affirmed them. I told him I felt as though I must tell the church that I belonged to Christ, and that my wife and myself were going to follow Him from this day forward.

He graciously allowed us the time to share this with the church. The outcome was so interesting. Some didn't believe we were real. They thought we were just doing this to gain favor with the court system. As if somehow this would change the judge's mind about what we had done. It was just as the voice had said, some would not believe. However, there were some—a small number of saints—who came to us and embraced us like only believers with the love of Christ can do. They began caring for us, holding us, and praying for us, helping us at every turn.

That night found our minds spinning with excitement, wonder, and zeal for Christ. God had lit a flame in our hearts for Him. We had been obedient to His call, and it felt so good.

Vonette and I could hardly stop talking to each other about what God was doing in our hearts. A great wave of hope began to wash up on the shores of our hearts. Could we have hope? Could we amount to something? Would we be productive again? The answers came rushing in like waves. I can do all things through Christ…I can do all things through Christ…I can do all things through Christ…. Wave after wave washed over our desperate hearts and souls.

Our love for one another seemed to be re-ignited. That night, love abounded—our love for each other and His love for us. It had been more than six months since we had been able to hope and love. Vonette and I went to bed with a peace that could only be explained by the supernatural. We embraced, kissed, and lovingly lay down to our peaceful night's sleep (something we had not had in a very long time).

While asleep, I had the most astounding dream. In fact, it did not seem like a dream at all, but perhaps a vision or some kind of being caught up in the Spirit. I don't know the mechanism God used, I just know it was His hand at work. It is impossible to share the fullness of my dream in words, but I will try to describe it as best I can.

In my dream, I was taken to a very large stadium at night, like a football or baseball stadium. We entered the stadium through a tunnel below the stands and moved to a stage area where the view of the inside of the stadium was totally blocked.

I did not know why I was here. I just sensed I was supposed to participate in this event. We then slowly walked up the stage stairs onto a very large platform. I now caught a glimpse of what seemed to be a concert stage, with people performing.

They were singing Christian music with thousands of voices joining them from the stadium, but I could not see them. I began really enjoying this back-stage experience, singing with them, loving the opportunity to praise our Lord. In just a few more songs, a man walked onto the platform, up to the podium, and began to speak. I moved closer and closer, so that I might be able to hear clearly. As I got within a few feet of going onto the open stage, I could hear him very clearly. What he was saying took away my breath.

He began to say that the person they had come to see was here, and he would be sharing what the Lord had done in his life—and would you please welcome Doyl Tully to the podium. He called my name, turned toward me, looking directly into my eyes with great expectation, and held out his hand as if to say, "The podium is yours!"

I was overwhelmed but seemed to understand that I had something to say, and I was there to say it. As I began to walk toward the podium, I looked out into the stadium, but the bright stadium lights made it difficult to see. The closer I got to the podium, the more I saw the thousands upon thousands cheering and applauding.

About the time I arrived at the podium, I woke up. The next morning, I shared the dream with my wife. I told her I did not understand everything about this dream, but I thought this was God's way of showing me that He wanted to use us in a very significant way for His kingdom. Even today, I believe that someday God will literally bring this dream to pass just as He revealed it to me.

God began to move mightily in our lives. He ministered to us through our new friends in the church. He also established special relationships that were strategic for our growth in Him.

The first relationship was with the pastor of the church. He was a young pastor with a big heart, a true love for Christ, and a willingness to spend time with us. This was very important in our walk because we still heard voices that would mislead us and stop our progress in the Lord. It was critical for us to have a godly person who would check our thoughts and desires. Although his heart was willing, his time was limited. We understood this, yet we prayed that God would lead us to someone who could spend time with us week in and week out. He did that very thing.

It was not long until a wonderful couple moved into town that fit our need to a tee. They were our age, and they loved God. In fact, he was called of God to become a full-time minister, but, so far, the timing was not right. Of course, God first wanted them to disciple us. It was such a wonderful relationship. Vonette could call her and talk, share, and pray together. I was able to meet with him on a regular basis to share and pray.

Another relationship came about because of Vonette's need to find work. She had gotten her real estate license and was pursuing that career, but then one day, the deacon's wife who lived across the street called. She had an upscale ladies' clothing shop and asked if Vonette would like to come and work for her. We could not believe anyone in this town would want to hire us, but God, being rich in mercy and grace, made a way where there seemed to be no way.

Because of this, we began a warm and loving relationship with this woman and her husband. This was exactly what we had prayed for. God answered our prayers.

Of course, we didn't know it, but this was only the beginning of a lifetime of godly relationships that the Lord would create for us. We now really began to grow in our knowledge of our Lord and our walk with Him. We had a hunger and thirst for God that nothing could satisfy except knowing Him more. He was alive to us. We were now poised for our journey with Jesus—to know Him more each and every day.

Even though our relationship with our Lord was soaring, the consequence of our sin had not gone away. It was hanging over us like an ominous dark cloud, threatening doom and gloom each and every day.

We had sought out the best attorney our money could buy. In fact, we spent our last bit of savings to cover his fee, thinking we would have no future if we lost this case and had to spend a possible fifteen years in prison. This incredible cloud of doom constantly pressed on me that on any day we could go to court, be found guilty, and end up in prison.

It was so difficult to carry this around. We were so young in our walk with Christ. We had every person who loved us praying that God would not let us go to prison.

Our attorney advised us to postpone our case as long as we could. Our hope was that as time elapsed, people might not care as much about what we had done. Our attorney reassured us that first-time offenders would not receive much, and that a woman would for sure get probation.

Here we were. Vonette was working for minimum wage at a small-town ladies' clothing store, and I was working in an upholstery shop making less than minimum wage. Everything in our lives except our walk with Christ seemed to be on hold.

We were headed nowhere, and I was not motivated to start anything. It did not seem to be worth the effort if it was only to be ripped from me later, depending on what happened with our case.

However, I sought some wise counsel, and after several sessions, I decided to return to college to obtain a degree. I would begin to work on a degree in computer science and see if this would work for me. I really did not know what all was included in a computer science degree, but it would be a start. No matter what happened to me later, what I accomplished in school could not be taken away.

So I started college. At first, I was driving one hour one-way, three days a week to take some of the basic course work. As I progressed into the degree program, I had to be there five days a week because of the math class work that was involved.

I will never forget those first few months. The Lord had told me to clean up and clean out my thoughts. Even though Christ was first in my life, I still had many problems that needed to be dealt a deathblow.

One of the first was my thought life. I found myself hating the law enforcement people for arresting me, hating the district attorney for wanting to prosecute our case to the fullest, and just hating my situation in general. This line of thinking was allowing Satan to feed my thoughts on a regular basis, and it kept me from experiencing the fullness of my Lord's communion and communication to me.

I went to work on this problem. I remembered reading in the Word of God that the Lord inhabits the praises of His people, so in my one-hour drive to and from school, I began to sing praises to God. One of the first songs I could remember was a song from my past named, "Do Lord."

I sang it loud, sang it soft, sang it real low, sang it high, sang with my head out the window. I would sing any way I could to fill my heart and mind with praises. By the time I reached school, I felt like I was going to be raptured. I was so full of Christ that Satan had no opportunity to fill my mind with wrong thinking.

Of course, later I learned new songs to sing. Also, friends gave us tapes that enabled me to fill my mind with both wonderful praise music and great sermons about our Lord. The point is that, over a period of time, this approach completely delivered me from wrong thinking. It enabled me to trust in my God for my future without blaming or hating others for the mess I had created. This was a very significant breakthrough for me, and I was then able to lead my wife through this thought process. I was greatly blessed as I simply obeyed the Lord.

Later on, the Lord began to convict me of our use of alcohol—whiskey to be exact. We were using it as a crutch to escape the reality of our troubles. At first, I began feeling guilty for going to church on Sunday, praising our God for His faithfulness and grace, proclaiming our faith in His abilities, and then coming home and drinking our high balls until we reached the mind numbness we needed to fall asleep. This began to bother me greatly. I knew I had to make a change. I talked it over with Vonette, sharing my conviction, and we made a decision to not drink at all on Sundays.

I must stop here and praise my loving and patient God. He took our very small step and blessed it as a step of obedience. He allowed us to feel good about this, and we felt as though we had obeyed our Lord. This is very important because we were committed to going God's way, but God knew just how much we were able to change at any one time.

This went on for a month or so until I began to feel that same conviction about drinking on Wednesday night after we attended our prayer meeting service. After several weeks of discussion, we agreed it was just like our Sunday stand and that we should not drink after we had been so intimate with our Lord. Praise God! We had made another step in the right direction.

This was good. We felt God's approval with this step also, and now we were only drinking on Monday, Tuesday, Thursday, Friday, and Saturday nights. I know you want to laugh, but I thought this was good.

Again, this went on for several months, and yet again the Lord spoke into my spirit about our drinking. At this point, I knew He did not want us to drink at all, but I struggled with that thought. Just as before, I tried to do something that would make me feel good about it, so I talked it over with Vonette and we agreed to drink only on Tuesday and Thursday nights.

This sounded like a great solution to me—one God would be pleased with. Surely He'd give His approval. But, this time it did not come. I still struggled. Every time I took a drink, conviction came upon me. I really did not understand why the Lord wanted me to quit completely. I thought just two times a week would be fine.

I will never forget what happened one Thursday night after several high balls. As I rolled over onto my arm to turn off the lamp on my nightstand, the Lord stopped me dead in my tracks. I saw my Bible on the nightstand, and a half-full, watered-down glass of whiskey sitting next to it.

God spoke directly into my heart and said, *"Did you read My Word tonight? Did you pray to Me tonight?"* I hung my head and sadly admitted I had done neither. I had to answer no to both questions. He then said, *"Choose which you want, the drink or Me!"*

In that very moment, I made a decision to choose Christ. I rolled on over, turned out the light in the room, and committed my life to Him in complete obedience. I would not drink any more. And I never did.

Some two years had passed since the time of our arrest. We had grown by leaps and bounds in our relationship with our Lord, but the dreaded court date finally came. Many were praying for us and believing by faith that God was going to deliver us from our troubles.

Our attorneys and many other people reminded us that first-time offenders—people like us—whose lives had changed would probably get probation. "Your life will go on," they'd say. "You can get past this." This was music to our ears; however, deep down, we could not shake the nagging possibility of going to prison.

As we went to court, our attorney began to maneuver with the district attorney about a plea bargain. He came back to inform us that he had reached a deal. We'd both plead guilty to possessing methaqaluade—which carried with it a maximum sentence of two and a half years in prison.

But he quickly followed this up with the promise that first-time offenders usually do not serve time, and women just do not go to jail under these circumstances. He advised that I should not worry about this, and take the deal. I could do some time—possibly two-and-a-half years—but I realized that two and one half compared to fifteen years was wonderful news. However, I did not like what I was hearing.

I was most concerned about Vonette. I could not let her go to jail. We had talked to people who had been there before and knew she would be raped within the first week of being there—I had to make absolutely sure she did not go!

I expressed my deep concern to my attorney, and he attempted to negotiate a better deal, but we were running out of time. He had done the best he could. Again, he assured me they would not send her to prison if I would only take this plea. He thought I might get something like six months.

Vonette pleaded with me to take the deal. By this time, she was ready to take the consequences and move on. So, after much resistance and concern, I yielded to this idea and prepared myself to plead guilty.

Now, understand that I knew I was guilty. There was no question about it, guilty as the day is long. I just wanted to protect my precious wife. So our attorney entered our plea, and the judge ordered a pre-sentencing background investigation to be performed.

During our sixty days of the pre-sentencing background investigation, those who loved and cared for us pleaded for our freedom. Many wrote letters to the judge expressing how we'd changed and did not need to go to prison. People from all over town signed a petition stating that they believed we did not need prison, that we were reformed. Some even made an appointment with the judge and begged him to give us probation.

I remember very well when this became a turning point in my hope. My mother told me about an appointment she had with the judge. She told him about the change Christ had made in our lives and that we truly were different. She explained that we were now able to live in society without the threat of doing drugs.

The judge fired back in a sarcastic sneer, "If they really have Jesus, then they will make it. Prison will be a snap." My mother wept. Reality began to set in that I would probably do some time. Of course, all our friends tried to encourage us to remain optimistic, but something did not feel right.

It was not long before we were brought before the judge. I will never forget the helplessness that raced over my body and heart. I was totally in the hands of another man—my future, my deliverance, my hope.

At this point, he asked me if we wanted to say anything. I did. I explained that we had received Christ as our Savior and Lord and that we were no longer the same as before. I shared that I was sorry for my sin and for breaking the law. I told him I hoped someday to be able to help others not go down the same path.

I saw the judge take a pen and scratch out something on a piece of paper, then write something new in its place. I had no idea what he was doing, but later I found out that he was intending to give the maximum sentence possible, until I spoke. He then changed his mind and reduced it.

He looked over his glasses at me and said, "Doyl Tully, for the crimes you have committed, I sentence you to fifteen months hard labor with the Department of Corrections."

I was stunned. Where was the grace for the first time offenders…or the six months…or the probation? My head swirled.

The judge then called Vonette to the same spot where I was standing and asked her if she had anything to say. She was so overcome with emotion that she could not say anything.

He then looked down those same glasses and said, "Vonette Tully, for the crimes you have committed, I sentence you to fifteen months hard labor with the Department of Corrections."

What? This could not be true! There had been some type of a mistake. This was not supposed to happen. My mind and heart was screaming, *Take it back…change your mind…God where are you?*

I cannot describe the hopelessness that ran through me. It seemed as though God had abandoned us. I felt all alone. Of course, we appealed this sentence immediately, which kept us from going to jail that moment.

I went home, walked into the backyard, lifted my face toward heaven, and screamed at the top of my lungs, "Why God? You know we do not need to go to prison. We are changed people. Why? Why? Where are You? Help me!"

I soon made an appointment with my good friend and pastor. As we talked, he spoke to me about how there are consequences for our sins. He shared the story of David and Bathsheba, and how David paid the price for his sins.

I did not like what I was hearing, but I began to realize there would be consequences for our sin, beyond what I was thinking. I did not like this answer. With us both being sentenced to go to prison, we were in a whirlwind of confusion.

During this time of confusion, one night Vonette was disturbed in her spirit and could not sleep. She got up from our bed and picked up her Bible simply to read for comfort. However, like many times when we do not know what to do, if we will but turn to the Word of God, He will speak.

The Lord led her to a verse that changed our lives forever. I do not think she fully understood the power of this verse. She just began to embrace that God was in control. It was Romans 8:28, "And we know that God causes all things to work together for good to those who love God, to those who are called according to *His* purpose." This was a powerful verse that we would claim many times in the difficult days to come.

SIN USHERS IN CONSEQUENCES

> However, because by this deed you have given occasion to the enemies of the LORD to blaspheme, the child also that is born to you shall surely die.
>
> —2 Samuel 12:14

We were convicted felons, sentenced to fifteen months hard labor with the Department of Corrections. We couldn't put that thought out of our minds. It was present every waking moment and even in our dreams. It was like a ball and chain around our legs, keeping us from moving in any direction.

This was a difficult time in my spiritual life. I questioned God. Why was He letting this play out this way? He knew we did not need to go to prison. Our lives had changed—because of Him. So why was He letting this happen?

I knew I would not be able to live with myself unless I did everything in my power to keep my wife from experiencing the horror of prison life, so now we invested our hope and faith in our appeal with the court system. It wasn't that we did not trust God.

We did, but we were just overwhelmed with this never-ending threat of prison. I must do what I could. I had to do all I could to keep Vonette out of prison.

We did a lot of praying. Praying a really simple prayer, "Oh God, please do not let us go to prison." Many people came together, sharing our hopes and hurts. Our church family surrounded us with love and assurance that God would deliver us. No one knew how He would do it, just that God was in control.

I continued to attend college, my wife continued to work for the clothing store, and we kept hoping against hope that we would not go to prison.

Another year passed, and I was two days away from final exams during the first summer session of school in 1983. The school's secretary came to my classroom and told me I needed to call my wife immediately. I located the nearest phone and called her, and what she had to tell me was almost more than I could take.

She picked up on the first ring. She was crying—almost uncontrollably. I asked her to calm down and tell me what was wrong, but inside I knew. After she was able to regain her composure, she told me that we had received a letter from the State Court of Appeals. I felt the same way I did when I learned that my father had died when I was eighteen years old. There was a pit in my stomach, and I felt sick. Then she said it—our appeal had been denied.

She had called our attorney and asked him what this meant. He responded that it meant we had done everything we could do, and it was just over. The authorities could come and take us to jail any day now, any time, moment, or second. *We were going to prison to serve our sentence!*

She began to cry again and through the sobs muttered the frightened words, "You must come home at once." I responded, "I am on my way." My head and heart began to spin, along with my thoughts, *My God, I am going to prison...My God, my wife is going to prison…No God!…Why God?…You know we are different people. We do not need to go to prison. Help me, oh God!* I left everything behind and raced to my car to start the journey home.

Even though it is only an hour drive, it seemed like an eternity. Would they come and get her before I could make it home? I wept so much of the way home that I did not think I had any more tears left. I prayed all the way home that I would get to see her before they came for us. My spirit was so heavy, so much in despair, so alone, just hurting. I thought of what my sin had done to my wife and where it was taking me.

A coldness raced across my body. Thoughts of despair poured into my mind like a waterfall. I had to fight thoughts of running my vehicle into a light pole to end this pain.

Even though I felt as though I would drown in despair, God reminded me I belonged to Him, and I must put my trust in the God who controls all. This seemed to enable me to make the long journey home.

As I approached the house, I could not even pull into the drive because of all the cars that were there. Our church family had already responded to the cry of my wife and were there praying and comforting her. I believe that about thirty-five precious believers came to encourage and support our every need. As I came into the house, Vonette and I, along with a few very close friends, made our way to the back bedroom.

I will never forget this moment in our lives. All the hopelessness that seemed to try to push its way into our home could not enter. It was left outside. The prayers of the saints were waging war against our seemingly hopeless situation. Our home was filled with such a sense of trust, of faith, of hope in our Lord God Almighty. No matter what things looked like, God had not abandoned us.

God used my wife in a powerful way that night as we gathered in that back bedroom. The Holy Spirit quickened her heart to a special verse that we had learned not long before in our walk. It was Romans 8:28, "And we know that God causes all things to work together for good to those who love God, to those who are called according to His purpose." (NAS)

She climbed onto the bed with her Bible, turned to this verse, and read it out loud. Then she looked deeply into my eyes, almost like seeing into my heart of fear and doubt, and she said these words, "Look, if God is real, if all of His Word is real, then this promise is for us. It has to be…and we must claim it tonight."

At this point, I desperately needed something to hold on to. Something I could point to and say, "This is how I will make it through the next fifteen months of my life." I am not suggesting we understood everything about this verse, but just enough to claim it for our circumstances. We loved God. We belonged to Him. It must be true.

I began to cry, "Yes! Yes! Yes! I will believe!" Vonette and I agreed to believe God and just see what He might do. So that day we re-read this verse and committed our lives to God once again. We confessed that we did not understand everything, but we would trust Him.

This was a very hard lesson for us to learn: just because we had turned our lives over to God, it did not mean He would necessarily deliver us from our consequences of sin. We remembered our pastor teaching us the Bible story of David and his sin with Bathsheba. This story mirrored the lesson we were learning—there are significant consequences for sin. This was a principle of God that would not change. It was true when David was king, it was true for me, and it is true for us today.

This was a time of great struggle for me. I had much to praise God about, because I was allowed to make it home before anything happened to my wife. On the other hand, I did not know how all this was going to work out. I just could not see it, and yet I was facing it head on. We did not know what tomorrow would bring. It required trust like we had never trusted before. It required faith like we had never believed before. It required pursuit of God like we had never done before.

Alone, Broken, and Humbled

> I sought the Lord, and He answered me, and delivered me from all my fears.
>
> —Psalm 34:4

The first day had passed, and we had not gone anywhere. Could they have made a mistake? Would they just not worry about us? Knowing this was not true, we waited for the authorities to come take us away. We would hardly venture out, not wanting to be separated even for a moment.

We would try to encourage one another, but it was difficult. I had to beat back fear and concern with every hour that passed, praying that God would protect my precious wife from harm.

I was concerned that I had done the wrong thing in taking the plea bargain. However, I could not allow myself to dwell on this, or it would take over my being like a wave on the ocean shore. In this short period of time, God worked relentlessly on our faith in Him—faith in His ability to deliver us no matter how the circumstances appeared.

I believe we waited about a week for the authorities to receive the paperwork which outlined our rejection from the court of appeals. At this point, they called us on the phone and asked us to come by the jail so that they could fingerprint us and fill out required paper work. We were so naïve, we thought they would just fingerprint us, fill out some kind of paperwork, and then let us go back to our home. We were not ready for what was about to happen.

I set up the appointment, and we arrived at the jail on July 12, 1983, ready to fill out the paperwork, give our fingerprints, and then go home. Well, they put us into a room to begin the processing, and in walked an older man, wearing a straw hat. He had driven up from another part of the state to process us. God was at work again for this man was a Christian. He encouraged us and prayed for us. What a comfort. What a blessing. God was with us, even in jail.

They completed our paperwork, took mug shots, fingerprinted us, and then strip-searched us. This was not, get a few things accomplished and then go home. We were here to stay. At least, stay until they could make room in the prison.

After the search, they brought us together one more time. Now the most difficult time had come—we were to be taken to our cells. This had to be one of the greatest testings of my faith—when they took Vonette out the door to take her to a cell. She went one way, and they took me another. My heart broke into a million pieces. No, it seemed to be ripped from me. I would not be there for her, to encourage her, to protect her from harm, to hold her. She was gone. Gone! Because of my own selfish sin, the one that I love most on this earth was now taken from me. My thought was, *Oh God, how can I bear this?*

The guard walked me back toward the cells where the air was cold as ice. A sense of evil blanketed the hallway. As we turned into the hall that would take me to my cell, men were hurling profanities, requests, and insults. They were calling out, "Fresh meat!" "He's mine!" and other obscenities. My heart raced as I realized this was no game.

I was placed in a maximum-security cell that would hold two inmates. The cells had concrete floors that were black with grime, cinderblock walls with graffiti covering every square inch, a concrete ceiling, and metal bunks each with a thin mattress and one blanket. There were absolutely no windows at all. There was a shower, a toilet and sink combination (sink directly above the toilet), and a small writing tabletop made of stainless steel.

As I spread my blanket over my bunk, thoughts raced through my mind. *How am I going to survive this? How is Vonette going to survive this? Oh God, You must help us. We cannot do this without You!*

About that time, my silent prayer was broken by the guard opening my cell door, throwing a new guy's stuff into the middle of the floor, and then pushing this tall, muscle-bound man into the cell with me. The guard barked out the man's name and said he would be with me for a while. I tried to collect my thoughts. I did not know what to say or how to act. Fear gripped me.

Since it was late afternoon when I was placed in the cell, it was not long until the guard made an announcement for all prisoners to make their way to the big room in their section for our evening meal (if you could call it that). I had no appetite, but I had no option either, so I followed the others into the larger room, not really large by any stretch, maybe 15 x15, with a picnic style, stainless steel table and benches, and a very large Plexiglas window that looked out into the main control area that all cellblock halls connected to. This would later prove to be a wonderful feature.

All the prisoners, about twelve or so, in my cell block crowded into this room. Many of them had tattoos all over them, and some of these tattoos communicated who their gods were, and they were not Jehovah. They all stunk to high heaven and were rude, crude, and very unattractive people. I don't mean they were ugly, just that the way they presented themselves reeked of indifference, coldness, and evil.

I knew no one. There was a great deal of tension in the room, and a great deal of fear on my part; however, I tried not to let it show. I tried to act cool and calm. Even though I was sure they all knew I was scared out of my mind. I had never in my spiritual life sensed so much demonic activity. Satan and his demons had full rule and reign in this place—until now. God had a representative who could and would make a difference, but I needed time to collect my faith.

As they served the evening meal through the hole in the door, I made a friend (at least for the moment) by refusing to eat my food and giving it to the first person who asked for it. After the meal, we remained in the big room for about an hour, and then we were herded back to our cell for the night.

I did not sleep much at all that night. I read the Word of God until we had lights out. Then I began to pray, pray, and pray some more. I knew this was going to be a journey, and the only way I would reach the other side was if Christ was in my boat. So that night I prayed that no matter what things looked like, I would put my young faith in Him. This was going to be a trial like I could never imagine. A trial created by my own sin. An experience God had ordained we must go through, not that I liked to think that way, but there it was.

One of the most difficult parts of our jail stay was an event that took place every day. Each and every day, the guard would come walking down the cell block hall, calling out a prisoner's name, saying, "Get your stuff together. You're going down the road!" The phrase, "going down the road," communicated that you were leaving for the state prison. This great fear loomed every day. Would he come today and say, "Doyl Tully, get your stuff together. You're going down the road"? Would he come and take Vonette to the state prison for women?

Oh, the agony of waiting, listening, hoping *not today*, praying to be spared this experience—but knowing it was just a matter of time before a bed in the state prison would be freed up, and I would go. Vonette would go. We knew this, yet somehow, we hoped against hope it would not happen. It would take divine intervention to prevent the obvious from happening. It would take a miracle. Each day that passed was a victory, but quickly it would flow into the fear of tomorrow. Would tomorrow be the day I would "go down the road"?

Chapter 6

CHALLENGED, BUT SEEING GOD

Behold, the eye of the Lord is on those who fear Him, On those who hope for His lovingkindness, To deliver their soul from death, and to keep them alive in famine.
—Psalm 33:18-19

Each day brought its own challenges. One of the most significant was the lack of communication with my wife. I longed to speak to her, to encourage her, to touch her…just to comfort her. But that was not allowed during our jail stay.

Over a little time, we learned the communication systems within the jail cellblock. At first, we had to bribe the privileged prisoner who served the meals, washed the clothes, and performed other tasks within the jail. He was a person who was trusted to freely roam within the jail blocks, performing the menial tasks that otherwise the jail would need to contract from outside.

The prisoner selected was nicknamed, Snake, and it fit. He was sly, manipulative, and very cocky, knowing he was the "chosen one." Trusting him was a fifty-fifty proposition. He would take your money, promise you anything, and then all you could do was hope for the best. Sometimes it happened, sometimes it did not. Like it or not, it was all we had, and I used him to the max.

I could write a letter to Vonette, and she in turn, could write to me. During our meal time, Snake would make the deliveries. This was so wonderful. I could sit down and read Vonette's words of care, love, and encouragement. It was a wonderful orchestra playing a love ballad with each letter that came. At times, her words praised God for His protection, and sometimes they were angry with Him for what seemed to us as abandonment. This would turn out to be our main way of communication while we were there.

Another form of communication came in a moment of creativity. Above the toilet was a vent that was covered with a grid. This vent led up into the attic of the jail. Once in the attic, sound could travel unrestricted. One night, after lights-out and desperate to hear Vonette's voice, I climbed up to the vent and called out to her. "Vonette, Vonette, can you hear me?" I waited. No response. I called again, "Vonette, Vonette, can you hear me?" Again, I waited, but this time, I heard her call out, "Yes!"

By now, the entire cellblock was up screaming for me to shut up. They made fun and yelled out names at me, spewing curse words with each breath, but I did not care. We had found a way to say a few words to each other, and that was all that mattered.

I never will forget one time while I was trying to talk to her through the vent, the men of the cellblock again began to log their complaints, but out of nowhere, the leader of the cellblock got everyone's attention and demanded that they all shut up and let us talk to each other.

From that day forward, the other prisoners began to respect our time to speak a few words each night after lights were turned out. It almost became a concert that the other men looked forward to—me calling out to Vonette and simply telling her that I loved her and missed her, and her calling back that she loved me and was praying for us. This was a great encouragement to us, and we were so thankful to our God for what seemed to be something so small in the eyes of others, but so great to our ears.

The next challenge I faced was in the area of sharing my faith. Again, I was probably in one of the darkest pits Satan could create. Darkness surrounded me, and I was the only light among them. The challenge to turn anything to a spiritual thought process was next to impossible. However, I believed that God had us there for a reason, and we were going to be busy about His business, telling others about Jesus. God blessed our meager efforts greatly. Before our stay ended, we led about half a dozen souls to know Jesus as Savior and Lord, held daily Bible studies, and discipled many to walk in Him.

The first time my cellmate was sent down the road, leaving me in a cell all alone, I began to rejoice with my new privacy and to feel so good about it. Of course, it was very short lived, maybe about four hours. This was a privileged time to let my guard down, to think without interruption, and a time to seek God alone, but soon it would end.

I was in deep prayer in my cell when the guard opened the door and pushed in a new cellmate, bringing a screeching halt to my spiritual focus. The guard told me that he had come from another cellblock within the jail, and that he had requested spiritual counseling from me. I was floored. But this was great news. My testimony of our God was spreading around the jail, praise be to God. Of course, I again had no choice.

I began a relationship with this man that started off innocently enough. He started to share with me his fears and problems. I counseled him in the Lord. He seemed to respond at first. I thought it was going great. Then items began to come up missing. First, it was small things that I did not care much about, but then it turned into larger pieces of my stuff. Finally, I needed to confront him with it. He got so angry I wasn't sure what he would do. I did not understand how to handle someone so out of control. At lunchtime, I claimed to be sick so I would not have to go into the larger meal room with him.

What happened next was more than I could have ever been prepared for. When it was time for all the cellmates to go back to their cells, I stepped out into the hall to get a change of pace. He stepped in front of me with this horrible look on his face. It startled me. I was not expecting this. I froze, waiting to see what would happen next. He began to move forward toward me, coming closer and closer. I noticed a shiny object in his hand. It was a homemade knife, called a shank. I thought, *My God, he is going to stab me!* He continued to move closer and closer, until he was one inch away from my face. One thing you learn quickly in jail is you never back up. If you show any sign of weakness, it will be exploited.

I stood my ground, not knowing how this would end up, but something strange happened. He stopped. His face was distorted into some unbelievable contortions, very, very weird looks—very demonic. His right arm was cocked and poised to run the shank deep into my stomach. It was like something evil had control of his person and being. He began to spew, as if trying to speak, but not able to. His veins popped out in his neck, head, and arms. He began to shake uncontrollably, like he was trying with all his might to stab me, but he could not get the hand holding the knife to budge.

I screamed out, "Get away from me!" (Not very spiritual, but it wasn't what I said, but Who I knew, that mattered.) No sooner had I gotten it out of my mouth, did he retreat to a corner of the hallway, continuing to spew obscenities at me, but looking as though he was some kind of whipped puppy.

In what seemed to be an hour, but really was just a few minutes, he screamed out for the guard. When the guard came, he requested that he be allowed to move into another cell with someone else. It was granted. I was saved. Looking back at this most dangerous situation, I believe that God dispatched His protecting angels to stand between this demonic threat and myself, and victory was mine.

Now by this time, we had been in jail about one and a half months. I was shaken by what had just taken place. I could only imagine what would happen when we got down to the prison. And what about my wife? What would they do to her? We had heard stories, and they weren't very hopeful. Truth is, I became discouraged. I needed a touch from my God. I just could not go on without some touch from Him.

I remember that night. I was alone in my cell because of the inmate that had just transferred. The lights were turned out at the normal time, and I made my way over to the vent to say my usual "I love you's" to Vonette. After completing our few words, I crawled into my bunk. I began to tell God that I just could not go on without something from Him. I did not know even what to ask for, I was just honest with Him. I needed Him that night. Not tomorrow or the next day, but right then.

Then I remembered the verse that says that God inhabits the praises of His people, so I began to praise God. It was so hard at first. I just said a few words. I had to really think hard for things to praise Him about, but I did. The more I did, the more praises I could think of, and the better I began to feel.

It was not long until this amazing manifestation took place. As I was praising the Lord in the totally dark room. Out of nowhere a very bright light began to descend, like a cloud, through the ceiling. It moved down, closer to me. The whole time I continued to praise my God. The more I praised, it seemed, the closer this bright light, or cloud, came. Finally, it completely engulfed me and my bunk. It is so hard to communicate what I felt. It was as though God came down from heaven and put His incredible arms around me and communicated so much love, warmth, and protection.

I stopped saying anything and just took this in. This went on for what seemed to be an hour, and then, the same way that the bright cloud descended, it ascended. Afterwards, I was so encouraged. I know to this day that the glory of God descended upon me and granted me a touch from my God. I never again became so discouraged while in the jail.

As the days passed (or should I say, as each minute passed which eventually turned into days passing), God continued to move in ways we just could never have imagined. One of these ways was through our church family. Some of our friends in our church body would come together and make the trip to visit the Tullys once a week.

Before their first visit, they requested a meeting with the Sheriff. In this meeting, the Sheriff determined that the best approach to allow all of these friends to visit Vonette and myself was to allow Vonette and me to come to them in a special room…at the *same time*.

The first time they came was such a wonderful day. The guard came to get me, telling me I had some visitors. I was glad to hear this and was very excited to know that some friends had come to visit me. This was going to be a good day.

Now, the normal visitation was in a very small room, separated in the middle with a half wall, half Plexiglas window with a few small holes for sound to travel through. It was cold, difficult to hear, allowed no touching, and was challenging at best—but it was better than nothing.

The guard began to escort me across the common area toward the entrance to the visitation room. Suddenly, a guard came with Vonette. It was so exciting to see her for the first time in such a long time. However, I still did not understand how special this day would become. The guard commanded me to stop right outside the door of a room just off to the side of the normal visitation room, which I would soon realize was the "special visitation room."

As we waited, I saw Vonette and her guard coming right toward us. Could this be? Could it be possible that we were going to be allowed to visit together with our friends? Surely not...not something this wonderful, no way! But it was. Her guard brought her to the same door, and we stood close to each other but were not allowed to touch. I wanted to reach out and just grab her and give her the biggest hug ever, but I couldn't.

In just a moment, the guard reached down and opened the door to the room, and to our surprise, there must have been about thirty-five people from our church family standing there. Some were cheering, some were crying, and some were jumping up and down with excitement. Vonette and I could hardly breathe.

The guard escorted us into the room, turned around, and exited the room, locking the door as he left. For the first time in over a month, Vonette and I were together and were able to embrace one another. Our friends were so loving. They held back while we embraced and held each other like never before.

After a time of this blessing, we were then able to greet and share with our dear friends from our church. The guards allowed us to have a thirty minute visit with our friends. It was so encouraging and uplifting.

Well, needless to say, this was not just a good day, it was a great day! One that I will never forget. From that day forward, because they realized God was using them to provide an opportunity for Vonette and me to be together, our friends made every effort possible to come visit once a week.

We always looked forward to these special times together with our friends. So many times they brought special things to us, like cards and letters, or a hamburger, or a candy bar, or just some gum. It all tasted so good. Several times they brought about fifty cards from the children of the Sunday school, all communicating how they loved us and were praying for us. I would read and re-read every one of these, and it was like a flood of love pouring into my heart. God used these special visits to underscore the importance of Christian friends, and how He uses these friends in difficult times to encourage and uplift our spirits. We will forever be indebted to these very special friends.

Another way God moved in our lives to encourage and demonstrate that He was there with us was a very special guard on night duty. His name was Chuck (not his real name).

I had not even noticed anything special about him to this point. He was nice, but just the "guard on the night shift." He came and went each night and did his job without any favor shown to us at all.

I guess it was about a month and a half into our term, when one night at midnight, the light was turned on in my cell, and Chuck opened my cell door. He stepped in and told me that they wanted to talk to me. I was so disturbed. I had no idea what "they" wanted. I got up, slipped on my jeans, and followed him out, not knowing where or what this was going to lead to.

We moved down the hall toward the guardroom. Right before we got to the guardroom, he stopped me. He told me, "right in here." Nervously, I opened a door and entered a side room. In the center of the room was a table with two chairs sitting at it. I was instructed to sit down.

By this time, I was praying under my breath that God would show me favor and deliver me from whatever was going to happen. I sat down expecting some kind of abuse, but much to my delight and surprise, Chuck, asked me a question. He said, "Do you like to play Battle?"

I thought, *What?* Battle…um. I replied, "What are you talking about?" He laughed and said, "You know, the board game called Battle."

I can't describe the relief that raced across my mind. I hadn't played that board game since I was a young boy, and to be honest, I really didn't care that much for it. However, tonight I loved it. I told him, "I enjoy playing Battle."

For the next three hours we played the board game and had a great time. I also began to ask Chuck about his life. Guess what? He was a Christian. God had sent a Christian guard to be some relief to the desperate environment that we were placed in. So many times in our Christian walk, we think we are the only ones in the midst of darkness, yet God has His people in places you would least expect it. Chuck was sent by our God. Our relationship grew, and over time, he helped us many times.

One particular time was when Chuck and I were playing a game one night, or should I say, early in the morning. It was after about two months of being separated from Vonette, and I shared with him how lonely I was—how much I missed being with my wife.

That night, he rose from the table, got his keys, and moved through the jail halls quietly and quickly. Before I knew it, he appeared in the room with my wife. I could not believe it. What was going on? What was he doing? He told us that we could have about an hour together, and that he would leave us alone. We could not believe our ears. It was the first time I was able to hold her the way I wanted to since that awful day we arrived. This was heaven on earth. All because God cared for us. He sent Chuck to help and be our agent of His blessing. This was not something that could happen often, but it occurred a couple times over the next month, bringing intense encouragement to our hearts.

DELIVERANCE IS SWEET

This poor man cried and the Lord heard him, and saved him out of all his troubles.
—Psalm 34:6

By now, it was September. We had been incarcerated for over two months, but it seemed like two years. Each day had settled into a rhythm.

We would awake, wait for breakfast, and then spend time in the common area. If everyone was good, we would enjoy this privilege for an hour or so. It was during these times that I would hold my Bible studies.

After this, we would be ordered back into our cells, and then came the dreaded call to "get your stuff together. You're going down the road!" The fortunate ones, who did not go, would settle into the wait-for-lunchtime mindset. During this time I'd do some personal study and reading in the Word.

After lunch, if everyone had been good, we would have one more opportunity to gather in the common room to pass the time. I spent this time in one-on-one discipleships of men who really wanted to grow in their walk with Jesus Christ.

Again, we would be herded back into our cells to wait for dinner. Once dinner was over, I would dive into a good Christian book or a study of a particular book of the Bible. This would last until lights out, at about eleven. It was so helpful for me to saturate my heart and mind with God's Word.

On his next visit, our pastor informed us that he had been talking with the state representative about us. He had heard of something brand new going on in the state legislature that just might help us get out of jail and prevent us from going to prison. Wow! Our jaws dropped onto the table. We could hardly believe our ears. What did he mean? We might be released?

Our pastor asked us not to get too excited but told us he was very hopeful that something would happen within a week. We left this meeting so encouraged and excited. We could not help ourselves. This was the first time we seemed to have promising news about being released. God was so good!

Each day now seemed like a week. We tried not to let it get to us, but we wanted so much for this to happen. I called my mother, and she actually talked to the representative as well and was very hopeful.

As the days accumulated, we found out more about this new program, but the news was disturbing instead of encouraging. We found out that this was a new work-release program for the State of Louisiana. It would be offered to only two first-time offenders of non-violent crimes. We qualified. This was the good news.

However, we faced two very difficult problems—problems that only God could cut through and make happen for us. First, the state legislature was still working on approving the program. In fact, the funding for this program was not even appropriated, and no one could tell any of us when that might happen.

Second, on top of the first bad news, we found out the number of eligible prisoners for the program was about 2,500 in the current prison system. 2,500 prisoners eligible! I could not believe it. How in the world would Vonette and I be selected out of that many people?

Our hope quickly turned into despair, and the days turned into weeks. We began to question if this would ever happen for us. After some time had passed, the Lord spoke a verse to us. The same verse He had spoken months ago, "All things work together for the good of those who love God...." Well, we loved God, and we believed we were called unto His purpose. As we held onto His promise, a surge of faith again began to build within our hearts.

Our pastor and my mom never gave up. They petitioned the Lord (and anyone who would listen to them) about us. They worked so hard on our behalf. On October 6, 1983, we got word that we had been selected for this new program!

Chuck came excitedly down the hallway, saying that they had just received a fax. The fax confirmed it. We had been selected for this new work-release program. There were no other details, but that we would not be "going down the road!" We would finish the remaining sentence in this new program—not in prison. This was incredible news!

He then raced over to speak with Vonette, and she, too, was overwhelmed. We could not believe it. We wanted to, but our hopes had been crushed before. We tried to protect our emotions, but we could not. That night, we could not eat or sleep. The anticipation of deliverance was so thick that we could slice it with a knife.

The next morning came, and not without notice, for I had hardly slept at all. After the breakfast call, but before it was served, a guard came to my cell, and told me to get my things together—we were going to be sent to Shreveport, Louisiana, to a halfway house! This would begin our work-release time…together.

It seemed God had parted the sea of the Department of Corrections, and we walked through on dry land. God had protected us, had saved us from prison, and delivered us into a program before the funding had even been set up. What a great God! We never stepped foot into a prison, but by all of man's wisdom, we should have. "But God, being rich in mercy and grace..." He delivered His children, and we began a new journey.

I will never forget that day. It seemed like the entire jail was excited. The other prisoners in our cell block cheered, the guards smiled, and Vonette and I were overjoyed, but I couldn't forget our friends.

Our church friends, who had been praying for our release and protection, came to see us off to the new program that would take us out of town and out of their touch, but not out of the touch of our Lord.

Well, it was a grand day! The cellmates cheered and shouted, "You did it!" The guards shook their heads in disbelief that we were not going to prison, but that's not all that happened to celebrate our transfer to the halfway house.

On that very day was the homecoming parade for the local high school. When we walked out to be transferred to the halfway house located in Shreveport, the parade was moving right in front of the jail. As we stepped out into the sunshine for the first time in three months, the high school marching band was passing by, playing a wonderful marching song that was to us, a divine message of God's joy in our release, helping us to celebrate this awesome time. It was like God was saying, *"I sent this to you so that you would know that all of heaven is rejoicing with you today."* That is the kind of God we serve!

There is so much that God did and revealed to me during our three-month stay in the jail; however, nothing like the intense personal relationship with Him that was established. Up to the time of entering the jail, Vonette and I both had depended a great deal on our Christian friends to help us understand what God was doing, saying, and what steps we should be taking.

When I entered the jail, the dependence on my friends was completely severed. I was thrust into an environment that demanded that I depend on my God for everything. The only other choice was to just abandon Him.

Everything else was stripped away. I only had the Word of God and my intimate relationship with Him—and it *had* to be intimate. I desperately needed to see Him, to hear His voice. I couldn't survive without His protection, His comfort, His hand, His encouragement, His presence, His direction.

During this time, God revealed to me that all I really needed was Him. He was, and continues to be, my shield, my rock, and my fortress...In Him will I trust. Him alone. This was what God was really doing in me during this time in jail. He wanted to place me in an environment where I must depend on Him only.

So many times before I went to jail, I would pray that God would not allow this to happen. "I do not need to go to prison," I proclaimed. Now I know that without this experience, I would have never matured to the walk I now have in Christ. Therefore, praise be to our Lord and God for all the jail time I served, for it was created by His divine plan, guided by His divine hand, and given for His divine purpose in me. Hallelujah!

The trip to Shreveport was a bag of mixed emotions. We were placed into the back seat of a deputy's car. He was nice enough to remove the handcuffs that we were wearing, and as we pulled out of the jail, several of our friends lined the parking exit, shouting praises to our God and cheering us on to a new season in our life.

The cheering did not stop there. For as we came close to the interstate that would take us out of town, again some of our friends from church were lined up, overjoyed at how our God had delivered us from one of our greatest fears.

After we had traveled over two hours into the journey, we saw something out of the front window that we could hardly believe. Some special friends whom God had used to disciple us were parked on the side of the interstate, holding a broomstick through the sunroof of their car. Attached to the broomstick was a large yellow ribbon and a sign that read, "Praise God for Doyl and Vonette."

I began to shout to Vonette, "Oh, my gosh! Look! Look!" The deputy, realizing what was happening, graciously pulled over so we could greet our friends. It was a joyous few minutes. After we returned to the car, we began to weep uncontrollably, embracing each other in the back seat, wondering what wonderful chapter would now be written in our lives by our great God.

We arrived at the Fellowship Mission and Halfway House late in the day. The mission was a run-down old hotel in one of the older parts of the city. On the outside hung a sign that read, "Jesus is Lord." And that He is!

The owner/director of the mission along with his staff met us at the door. The owner had purchased it when it was about to be condemned, and he was in the process of renovating the inside. The mission stood about five stories high and was a grand old building that definitely had seen its better days.

As we entered the building, what a reception! We instantly smelled something in the air. I was not sure what it was, but it had a foul, musky smell to it.

On the first floor was the entrance, a gathering room along with the kitchen and dining area, and a couple meeting rooms. The hotel rooms were located on floors two through five, accessible only by a staircase in bad need of repair and refurbishing. Only the first and second floors had been made functional. What I mean by functional is running water (hot only sometimes), rooms with a bed, a working kitchen, and folding tables for dining. I believe God had to be in this mission in order for it to be approved for opening.

The director, as well as the staff, was so excited to see us. They greeted us with almost celebrity status. Not like movie stars, but just the idea that never before in the State of Louisiana had a program like this ever happened. We were the first two prisoners ever released by the state correctional system into a work-release program established at any halfway house. The director took us right up to his private quarters, asking us all sorts of questions. He offered the use of a phone, food, and anything to help us settle in.

We were overwhelmed. We faced such a huge challenge. We were incredibly thankful for our release, but having been locked up for about three months, our psyches were damaged and distorted. We felt uncomfortable around others. We just couldn't interact as normal people. It was very difficult to know what to say or even how to act around others.

We wanted to fit in and be what the director wanted us to be, but it was difficult. We had no idea how important this was for the state, for Fellowship Mission, or how important it would become in our lives.

I finally asked if we could go to our room and try to get settled. We could face these new people tomorrow. We prayed that night. First, with thanks for God's deliverance and then that God would strengthen us to be used for His kingdom, however that was to be. We slept well for the first time in a long time.

The next couple days proved to be enlightening to us. It began with the director awakening us and asking us to dress and meet him downstairs. I looked over at Vonette and commented, "Well, so much for settling in!"

At the meeting, the director began to share that he had been praying for people like us to begin this new program. For years, he had been one of the authors of legislation to create a work-release program for first-time offenders who had been engaged in a non-violent crime. He had been lobbying legislators for years, hoping the state would pass and fund this, which then would help fund his mission, enabling him to reach and serve even more people in the name of Jesus Christ.

He went on to share that without this funding from the state, he was sure the mission would not be able to stay open, but now, the state was moving on it, and we had become the *first* of what he hoped to be many to follow.

He began to tell us how important it was for us to make this work. We could literally become the salvation for the mission. He challenged us to not mess it up, but in every way to become a model for others to follow, so the state could see that this could work. Wow! Talk about pressure. We didn't know what to say, except, "With God's help, we will do our best, and you can be assured, we will not mess up."

At that, he informed us of our scheduled events and activities for the coming weeks. You would have thought we were something to see. He had churches lined up for us to share our testimony with and raise funds for the mission. State representatives were coming for luncheons where I was to speak and share our life with them. Radio and television interviews were set up, and on and on.

We were thrust into a limelight we were not ready for in the natural, but we served a very big God. He began to work in and through our hearts, giving us everything required of us. Remember, we were still young Christians who desperately needed someone to disciple us. We prayed fervently for this, and God provided—He is Jehovah-Jireh!

The next day was again very demanding, full of meeting people for the purpose of raising money for the mission. This was going to become a regular occurrence over the next several months, and as we did more of this, it got easier. We so much wanted God to use our testimony to turn people to Him, because He is the answer to anyone's needs and problems. The more meetings, the more I was able to share about my Lord and His great deliverance in my life.

On about the third day after arriving at the mission, I walked into the director's office at his request for a meeting. Sitting in a side chair, just off to the left of the director's desk was a man, I would say in his fifties. As I walked into the office, this man hopped out of his chair and thrust out his hand as if to cut though any hesitation I might have to embrace him.

He was dressed in a plaid shirt with khaki pants and a large pair of suspenders. He was a sizeable man, and he needed the suspenders because his stomach far exceeded the average size of a waist, but he also had this unbelievable countenance and smile.

Grinning from ear to ear, he began to speak, "Hello, my name is Bob Hannigan, and it is good to finally meet you." I put my hand out to go through the motions of a handshake, but he grabbed it with excited firmness and gave me a real manly handshake. *Well, I wondered, who in the world is this guy?*

For a few minutes, he asked me questions, and I gave general responses. There was something different about the guy. Something I could not seem to put my finger on. He was using Jesus' name and talking about how great our God is…there was just something that seemed to be drawing me into this moment.

He finished his questions, and then asked me if Vonette and I would like to attend a Bible study that he was leading that night with his wife. Well, before I knew it, I had said yes and then wondered why. Why would we want to go to a Bible study with these old fogies? Oh well, it would just be one time.

That evening, Vonette and I were apprehensive about the trip. We had not gone anywhere much since before we entered jail. For that matter, right now, we did not even like to be around people, and here we were going to a Bible study with these old people who we would have nothing in common with at all. I told Vonette that we just needed to push through this, and I promised not to let it happen again.

We met Bob and his wife, Pinky, downstairs that night, loaded up in their car, and headed to the Bible study. We made small talk on the way, and they seemed very genuine, very nice, and they were Christians. A different kind of Christian…real people and real Christians.

God seemed to be so real to them. Jesus had made a difference in their lives. Boy, did we have a surprise when we arrived at the study. We walked into a home filled with young couples our age. They had gathered together in Jesus' name to listen to a dynamic, Spirit-led Bible teacher, none other than Bob.

He opened up the Word of God and began to teach like I had never heard before. The Spirit of God seemed to give him so much enlightenment that I could not take it all in. The wisdom of God rolled off his tongue like a huge boulder rolling down a hill—truth after truth, wave after wave—pounding into our hearts and souls.

We were so hungry, in such need to hear from God's Word that this was like a waterfall of truth flowing across our spirits. God had answered our prayers for someone to disciple us and teach us the things of the Spirit. We were so thankful for Bob and Pinky. This began a relationship that remains to this day, some twenty-three years of being together.

He often refers to us as his spiritual son and daughter, such an awesome thought when you think about it. A thought that was modeled in the Old and New Testaments. Elijah and Elisha in the Old and Paul and Timothy in the New, this was a divine relationship taking place by the hand of God and continuing to this day.

God did so much in our lives during this time. Little did we understand that He was preparing us for much more to come. We were just trying to be obedient in every area. If He wanted to use us by sharing what He had done in our lives to fund a mission, that was just fine with us.

I grew quickly in understanding how to share my testimony. I had to learn to be prepared to share for just a few minutes or as much as one hour. Many people were being blessed by hearing it. In fact, people were giving their hearts over to Christ after hearing what God had done in our lives. This was such a blessing to us.

After we had served five months of our fifteen-month sentence, we were paroled by the state, and our time at the mission came to a close. We now would move out into an apartment and begin to live a more normal life, only reporting to our parole officer on a regular time schedule.

Of course, Bob and Pinky were there with us every step of the way, nurturing us, teaching us, guiding us, and caring for us. We joined the church they attended, and we were there every time the doors opened. We sat under Bob's teaching in a Bible study class and soaked up the Word of God on a weekly basis.

I secured a job and was able to make a living during this ten months. God used it to teach us and to allow us to acclimate back into a life of freedom. After the ten months had passed without incident, we were released from the state. It was over. This was such a blessing. Finally over! We had walked through on dry ground. God had met us at every step of the way. Surely God does bless obedience—a lesson He would highlight throughout our lives.

I made a decision to look into returning to school and completing my degree in computer science. I would need to return in January of 1985 with the hope of only one year of work remaining. We were hoping that this would reestablish us for the future. It would require sacrifice. Vonette would need to work hard and help support our home. She was more than willing.

Finally, after serving five months of a sentence in jail, the halfway house, and then ten months of probation, we would begin to do something for our future. We weren't sure what, but we had grown much, God had taught us through Bob and Pinky, and now we were ready to move forward with our lives.

THE BEGINNING OF A NEW LIFE

> Therefore we have been buried with Him through baptism into death, so that as Christ was raised from the dead through the glory of the Father, so we too might walk in newness of life.
> —Romans 6:4

Like seasons come and go, winter moving into spring with such radiance, splendor, and promise, so our lives were transitioning. The death of the intense and hard winter of our consequences was beginning to cry out with hope.

Vonette and I had discussed many times, "What should we do?" We had talked about many things, such as staying in Shreveport and developing some kind of career, although we were not sure what this could be, given our past. Who would want me, or her, for that matter—convicted felons!

This was a very challenging time in our faith. We were praying and asking God to speak, but were very unsure what His will would be for our lives. We understood that we were in a place where spiritually we were growing by leaps and bounds. Moving out of this context did not seem to be a good answer; however, there was no real direction to stay. There was no voice giving guidance—no visions, no real steps revealed. We just wanted to know that we were in His perfect will and moving in His provision.

So, we were in constant prayer. One day Vonette had the thought that I should return to college and finish my degree. What a great thought, but next to impossible. We'd have to move to Monroe, Louisiana (where my school was located) and find a job. I'd need to be accepted by the college, which was not a sure thing by any means. Plus, I'd have to re-engage my mind in the intense mathematical and computer science course work. It was staggering—almost too overwhelming for me at this point in our social rehabilitation and spiritual development.

However, God used Vonette at this time in our lives as she gently but firmly encouraged me to give God a chance to reveal this to us. So, we agreed that several things must happen: I must be accepted by the school, I must have money to go to school, I must find a job to support us, we must secure a place to live, and we must know and agree together that this is God's will for us. On top of all of these difficult requirements, we decided they must be all met within six weeks, because that is when the January session began.

We asked God to reveal His perfect will in all these areas. This was an amazing time as we waited each day, anticipating seeing God move in some way. We were excited at times, anxious at times, and sitting on pins and needles at times.

I want you to know that God got busy and gave us incredible direction, almost like lightning bolts from heaven, overpowering all obstacles and barriers. I cannot express what a powerful message He sent to us during this most fragile time in our lives. We were not sure what our future would be, could be, or even what we wanted it to be. God seemed to say, *"Now that you have given over the desires of your hearts and are willing to allow Me to move freely in your lives…watch what I will do!"*

And He did do all that was necessary and then some. Within two weeks, I was accepted by the college. In fact, the truth is, they embraced me with open arms and took me in as their project. Not only were they willing to allow me back to school to complete my degree in computer science, but they began working on my behalf to secure a grant to help with the first semester tuition and books.

To some, this was not a huge amount of money, but to Vonette and me, it was an impossibility. I had not worked very much, and the little I did earn went to support us during our stay at Shreveport. In others words, we were completely broke, and when you're broke, even a thousand dollars is an impossibility. However, we serve a God of possibilities, not impossibilities, and things continued to happen.

I will never forget the incredible temptation to trust in ourselves during this time. This was a temptation that produced a very difficult moment in my spiritual life. God was moving in the spiritual realm, and we sensed that something was happening, but we were unsure how it would play out.

A friend called and shared about a job in the town where the school was located. Our friend had prepared the way so that it would be for my taking. I would be with a medium-sized company, working with computers at night, a job workable with my schooling schedule. The pay would be much more than I could have even imagined. Our hearts and spirits soared! I was thinking that this was a miracle of provision from our God. It was a two-hour drive to the interview. I arrived and went in.

By this time, my God was so much a part of my life that I could not talk very long with people without bringing up His awesome work in my life. This interview was no exception. The man, very nice at first, seemed to become uncomfortable during the interview. I could not understand why until he began to ask me some pointed questions about my faith. He said, "Because you believe in God so much, how would you respond if someone cursed at work?"

Well, I was a little taken by this question. I told him I would handle it like I do in any situation. That people must choose how they live their lives and the way they speak. Well, that response did not seem good enough to him. So, he came back with another pointed question. He asked, "Well, if the others in the computer room began to curse in ways that used God's name in vain, how would you respond?"

Something grabbed my heart. It was like Satan himself was saying, "Yeah, you really need this job. Don't blow it! Tell him what he wants to hear. If you stand up for God, you will lose this job, a job you must have in order to move forward with your life. If not, you will not go to school. You will not amount to anything. You will not be able to provide for your family."

There was an instant and powerful battle raging inside me. My heart was staggered. My spiritual knees grew weak; however, I knew that I could not deny the personal and public relationship God had established with me. My faith, as small as it was (the size of a mustard seed), began to rise up into my mind and mouth, and I spoke with a nervous confidence at first, but as each word came forward, I realized this was not a job given by my God, but rather a test or a temptation. I was being tempted to compromise my beliefs with an ungodly world system and values. I told him, "I believe in the Most High God. I believe that Jesus Christ is my Savior, and I live, as much as possible, for Him, my Lord. For anyone to take His name in vain is an offense to Him and to myself, His child. I would quickly point out that offense and ask the person not to speak this way again in front of me."

Well, needless to say, the interview was over. As I stepped back into my car, I cried out to my God, "If not this way, what way?" The Lord spoke back, "Well done," and to me, this was all I needed to hear Him say. God was speaking to me that I had passed the test and that He had something else for us. Trust and obey, for there is no other way.

Upon my return, I shared with Vonette what happened, and it challenged us both. We were excited that I felt I had passed a test; however, the need loomed like a great cloud. How would God provide? Would He grant this need? We sought the Lord in prayer, and soon He revealed His way.

At the end of the third week, Vonette received a phone call from the school that said we were approved for a grant supplying my tuition and books for the first semester. We rejoiced in our God, but we were also puzzled about how I would secure a job.

Passively, Vonette shared this concern with the computer science department head. She shared that this was one of the most difficult pieces remaining and that it must be solved before we could commit. He simply said that he understood and hoped it would work out.

Well, later we would find out that he did more than that. Within another week, about four weeks into this, the department head called again—this time with incredible news. He would be willing to hire me as a computer lab assistant and pay me to go to school. Our God was so awesome!

Within just four weeks, God had provided just about everything we needed for my return to school. We now only needed a place to live. Well, that was no problem. Vonette traveled to the college town, and within one day found a nice, clean, two-bedroom house for rent that we'd be able to afford with my work and the job that she would find.

Now we just needed to agree together that this was God's will, which did not take us long. We saw again God's provision is not limited by man, or circumstances, or even our lack of faith. He can, and will, move whatever is necessary to enable His children to proceed in His will. We agreed and set a moving date.

Our lives would change. It would again be a new beginning. It would be a doorway that all of deity had created and placed in front of us to step through—and step, by faith, we did. Little did we know how much change was coming.

I began school with a passion and drive that was so intense, knowing that my God had placed me there. I studied as unto Him. I wanted to please Him and do my very best in everything I did. However, even with Him as my focus, the degree program was difficult and very challenging for me. It required a great deal of math and computer science course work.

I was now one full year away from my earliest possible graduation, and every course was very time-consuming, requiring my full attention. I would go to school each day because my math courses required five-day-a-week attendance. Then I'd work in the afternoons and evenings, and study until very late at night or even into the early morning. My life was consumed with school. There was very little time for other activities.

God continued to prove Himself to us. He provided a job for Vonette within a week of our move to Monroe. This was a tremendous blessing. We needed her income in order for all of this to work. God seemed to say, *No problem.*

As busy and challenged as we both were, Vonette and I made commitments to our Lord to attend church on Sunday mornings and to do whatever we could to share what God was doing in our lives. This commitment was important to us. We understood that God moves as we pursue Him, and we wanted to tell others about how He was working in our lives. We would not allow our situation to change this. Through all this, God provided a new reason for us to move forward, making sure we stayed on His course.

Only a few months into my return to school, Vonette began to be overly tired almost each day. She was struggling with nausea and a lack of energy. Of course, I told her she just had to pull herself up by the bootstraps and go to work; we really needed her income. She did, but she would return home from work needing to take a nap. Almost no energy.

Well, I guess I was clueless. I had no idea what was on the way. Vonette finally went to the doctor, and we were informed that she was pregnant. Wow! Not something we were expecting. Not something we had planned. Not something we had sought. How would this work out?

However, God chose the timing. He had decided to bless us with a child, and we were happy and excited about it. We were just not sure how it would all work out. The baby was due in September, but I would not graduate until December at the earliest. How would we provide for this new child when we were just barely providing for ourselves? How would we pay for the delivery of a child with no insurance?

So many questions without ready answers. Well, not answers that we had, but God used this time of unending questions to move us into more dependence on Him in every way. We knew we must completely trust in His provision and direction. We must not let up, but press in. We must trust even more, believing that He had all the answers to our questions, and time would reveal His provision.

We did have opportunities to share our testimony. Our church allowed us to communicate all of what God had done in our lives up to this point. It was awesome to see how God used our testimony. Over and over again, people were touched and changed as we shared of our God's loving care and provision in our lives.

It was during this time that I began to teach God's Word along with sharing our testimony. It was a feeble attempt, but one that was required for me to begin a journey of sharing the truths of God's Word. People were kind and gracious to allow me to stumble though teaching and, when needed, to simply say, "I do not know." I think they saw a genuine heart and desire to know God.

God used this time as the "stimulation to teach" in my life. It was not the call to teach, but just stimulation of His truths that seemed to change me, if no one else. This became something I enjoyed, liked, and wanted.

Now, understand, I felt totally inadequate to teach in any way, and I would begin each teaching saying so. But my heart wanted to know Him and His truths, so if I could squeeze it into my busy study schedule, I took the opportunities as they were offered. There weren't many opportunities, but enough to begin something in me that later became irreversible. (I just need to say here, that whatever opportunity comes, do your best to seize it. With God, it can lead to stimulation toward new and greater things for the future.)

Then, the great day came—when our firstborn came into this world. Benjamin Doyl Tully, born September 19, 1985, in Monroe, Louisiana. It was both a glorious day and a day of wondering. Wondering how God would make a way where there seemed to be no way. Wondering how this Benjamin, son of the right hand, would live out his life…

And wondering how I would be able to finish school. We did not have the money. I needed Vonette to work, and she was now unable for awhile, but God continued to move on our behalf. People we did not even know would show up on our doorstep and tell Vonette that God had spoken to them, telling them to bring by clothes or money.

Sometimes, people would show up with sacks full of groceries and leave them on our doorstep. We even had someone deliver a stove to our house because ours had gone out, and Vonette was trying to cook on a hot plate. This provision, what I call manna from Heaven, took place from September through December of 1985. This was the exact time of need, due to the birth of our firstborn son. Praise be to our God for His miraculous provision, again and again.

Thanks to the creative work and scheduling of my department head, it was almost December, 1985, and I was within sixty days from graduation. I was soaring in pride that my God had brought me so far.

But financially, we were a disaster. We had no money, and the one credit card we had was charged up to the max. We were not sure how we would be able to make it, even to the end of December.

I never will forget the events that took place next. My department head called me into his office. He was proud of my accomplishments. He was happy that he had invested in me and hoped that God had great things ahead for me. I was so excited and ready to move into the phase of looking for a great job, of making enough money to provide for my family, and of moving forward in this wonderful new life of serving my Lord.

I was just not ready for my department head's next statement. He said, "Get me your résumé, so that I can find you a job. You know, with your background, no one will want to hire you. I will try to go before you and get you into a position, so you can prove yourself." (That is, he was saying, I will beg for a job for you.) Companies were coming to the college to spark interest in students with good GPAs. My department head said he had spoken with several companies, and things were not looking good for me.

Now, I know he had good intentions, but—I was devastated! Did I move on the will of God, work so hard to achieve a good GPA, sacrifice so much, so that this man could go and beg for me? I was stunned, and just told him I would put a résumé together. My faith was being tested. I must say, at that moment, my faith seemed to crumble. This was on a Friday afternoon.

I went home after my classes and could not study or think of anything but his statement to me. My mind swirled with doubt. Vonette began to ask me what was wrong. After she put the baby down to bed, I shared what he had said. We cried together and were angry together. It seemed like all we had hoped for had just collapsed. What kind of life was really ahead for us? One of begging, or one of possessing? One of trusting in man's hands, or one of relying on the mighty hands of God?

That night and the next day were times of darkness. We struggled to trust in our God. It was as though not just a wave, but a whole ocean of doubt had come crashing in.

I'll never forget that next glorious Sunday morning when my wife awoke. She raised up in bed and cried out, "Doyl, wake up!" This was not just a call to wake up from the night's sleep, but more of a call from the spiritual voice of our faith. Let's wake up and see our God and who He is.

She began to express God's Word, God's awesome past provisions, His tender care for us, and God's plan and purpose that continued to be unveiled. Then she made a very profound and necessary statement. She proclaimed, "God has not brought us this far to have us beg for a job, or to let us go. Why don't you go back and tell this man that you want a list of every possible company the school has, and we will send out résumés and place our faith, trust, and provision in God for our future job."

With this magnificent proclamation and the light of Christ, our faith poured into our hearts like a river, and the darkness drained out like a sink of water after the plug's been pulled. Darkness fled. That Sunday morning at church was a special time of worship for Vonette and me. God seemed to smile upon us as we worshiped Him.

I went to school on the next day, excited but nervous. How would I share this? What would my department head think? Well, God had a unique way for this to come out.

I was working in the computer science lab that afternoon, and my department head came walking through the lab. There were students all around working on computer lab assignments, and I was helping them. As he walked in, something seemed to take over me. The Spirit of God surged within me, and after getting his attention I just shouted out, "Please, give me a list of all the possible companies, and I will send my résumé to them, and God will decide where I work."

Well, he was stunned. So many heard my statement. So many were hanging on the edge of their seats, wondering what he would say in response. I think he was so surprised that he was at a loss for words. He finally just agreed to give me the list, and later, Vonette and I went to work.

We sent out over one hundred résumés to companies. Any company, no matter what business they were in, even defense contractors, which required security clearances we were told would be an impossibility for me. We thought long and hard over each word we wrote in the résumé. We prayed for God to direct our every thought and give us the exact words we needed to write.

Then, in three weeks, the answers began to flow in. And guess what? These companies were asking to fly me out to their locations for interviews. Can you believe this? A convicted felon. A person some thought would need to beg for a job. Not just a request for an interview from one company, but company after company sent invitations to be interviewed at their home offices.

I began scheduling flights and conducting interviews with both regular business companies, as well as even the impossible, defense contractors. When all the dust had settled, I had five offers from both business and defense contractors from all over the country.

And by the way, this was the most offers any graduating senior had for that year. Not only that, I was offered the most money in starting salary of any graduate. My department head was in awe. My fellow students were amazed, and Vonette and I were again overwhelmed by our God's provision.

Now our only challenge was which job to take. We prayed and asked God to give us a way to know which job He wanted for us since all the jobs were good and the pay was almost exactly the same. We prayed that He would show us, in some way, which job to take. We only wanted the one He wanted.

Then we received the final offer from a company in Dallas, Texas. This salary offer was about twelve to fifteen percent more than any of the others. It was from a defense contractor, which others had said would be the impossible. We knew this was a sign from God, and we were headed to Dallas, Texas.

Again, I thanked God for my wife and her steadfast faith in our Lord. So many times without her, I would have crumbled under the testing of our faith, but God has so fused us together. We are as one. When one is weak, the other is strong. Thank You, Lord Jesus, for my mate for life.

Chapter 7

THE SHAPING OF A NEW LIFE

And put on the new self, which in the likeness of God has been created in righteousness and holiness of the truth.
—Ephesians 4:24

The move to Dallas began a new season in our life—one of constant provision. Finally, a season in which we could make plans to provide financial security. A time for us to live as a family, grow spiritually, and see what God had in store for us as a couple for His kingdom.

After we were able to settle into a church, which took months of looking and praying, God allowed me to begin to pursue my intense desire to teach His Word. Not necessarily only for others, but also that I might grow in wisdom and that I might know the depths of His unsurpassed knowledge and walk in His ways with confidence. This honors Him in every way.

We were attending a Bible study class in our new church and enjoying the people there; however, there was something inside me that was not satisfied. Every Sunday, I wanted to say so much about our God and the lesson. My wife told me I needed to stop talking and let the teacher lead the study. I told her that God had put His passion within me, and I could not keep silent! She responded, "Well, just don't talk so much." I agreed, but I could not stop.

The Spirit of God within me would not let me remain silent or even be happy with only attending a class. So, I approached the leadership of the Bible study and told them I would be willing to fill in if they needed someone to teach.

Well, the very next Sunday, I was called in after church and asked to take a singles' Bible study class. I eagerly said, yes! This was the beginning of a teaching career that continues to this day—1986 to now. Week in and week out, sometimes many times a week, I'm teaching God's Word to people who will listen to His truths. It is my calling and my passion—to teach the life-changing truths of God's Word. Nothing can take its place. Nothing can be substituted. Nothing!

God continued to grow us in Him. This Bible study class seemed to catapult us into ministry. The singles were so loving and welcoming to who we were in Christ. They embraced our desire and hunger for God. We seemed to feed off each other. We not only held Bible study on Sundays, but the singles were over at our house all the time. We loved on them, counseled them in their walk in Christ, built them up, and motivated them to be true to God during this challenging time of their lives. They loved it, and we loved it.

We also started a Friday night prayer time for the singles. They would come and gather at our house, and we would enter into a prayer time with the Lord. It started with just a few, but before long they were all over the floor, in the chairs, on the stairs, just all over the place, crying out to God.

It was like the Spirit of God would move from one to the other, impressing on them what to pray. Some confessed their sins, while others asked for wisdom, and some interceded for others. It was an awesome time of being together and seeking Him in pureness of heart.

I also started a Tuesday and Thursday 6:00 A.M. prayer time with three of our single guys. They would show up at our home at six in the morning, and we would talk about their struggles and pray over them, asking God to do great things in their lives. God moved so much during this wonderful time because of our intense pursuit of Him, and many of these singles were kept from the jaws of Satan and his schemes. One became a missionary, and others became great men of God.

We have learned that when God moves, you can expect two things to happen.

First, God will test our faith. We became settled into our singles ministry, and things were moving forward for the Lord. The hearts of our singles were intense and yielding to the Father. It was a very exciting time to be a part of this ministry.

One night, my wife and I said our goodnights and shared our usual goodnight kiss, drifting off into that sleep that comes quickly from a work- and ministry-filled day. I'd had a difficult day at work, not because of anyone, or my boss, or anything of the like. It was just that the intense software problem I was working on was eating my lunch, and my deadline was looming just around the corner. This was putting great stress on my work team and myself. We needed to press through the problems, and make the product work soon for our customer. When your customer is the government, it seems to add stress.

Also, we had a single come by our home at 6:30 P.M., and she was in such need. Vonette and I ministered to her until about eleven thirty, and sent her on her way encouraged in the Lord; however, we were tired and ready for a very deserved and needed night's sleep. I was rising early the next morning to catch a flight to Chicago for some project meetings with our customer.

From just after midnight to about 4:00 A.M., it was a wonderful, restful sleep, but then everything changed. I began to dream. No, not just a dream. I have had many dreams. The kind of dreams that

I was well aware were only dreams that made no sense and had no meaning, but this one was different.

I knew from the beginning it was a "God dream"—a dream God wanted to use to speak to me and communicate a message of importance and direction. All this was known in my spirit even though I was asleep and not in a conscious state.

Anyway, the dream went like this. I was walking up an inclined bank covered with very green grass and lush foliage. Trees were all around and so beautiful. As I arrived at the top of this bank, I saw the most beautiful sight I had ever seen. It is impossible to describe the beauty that existed in my mind.

I saw something like an emerald lake, like a mirror that was sparkling from the rays of the sun. Around the lake were plants and trees that were so lovely and beautiful that only the Divine could have created them. They seemed to beckon me into the lake.

I stood there for a few minutes trying to take it all in. I was experiencing such peace and joy. It rushed over my soul like a waterfall, exploding into my heart and pushing out any concern, stress, or anxiety that existed in me. It was like heaven was on earth. I was caught up into some place that had to be created by my God. I remember the joy that overwhelmed me, causing me to smile and laugh quietly under my breath.

Well, something called out to me to jump into the lake. I just knew I was to dive in. In fact, I wanted to. I wanted the waters to engulf me. So, I removed my shoes and dove on in. Well, I was somewhat surprised at the consistency of what I thought was water. It looked like water, but it didn't act like water. I could swim in it and dive under it and back up to the top effortlessly. There was no concern about sinking or drowning if I did not swim. In fact, if I stopped swimming, I wouldn't sink, I just remained buoyant. I could breathe easily above and below the water. I was enjoying all this immensely.

I came to a stop and began to look around and take it in when suddenly something came up out of the water some fifty yards away. It was hard to see all the details from that distance, but it was not something I wanted to be in the water with me. It was snake-like, very large, and horribly ugly.

I thought I'd have enough time to get out of the water before this thing could get to me, but about that time, it plunged underneath the water. I just knew it was coming my way. In what seemed to be just a moment, it traveled under the water and surfaced again at about twenty yards away from me.

This time, I could see it clearly. It was very snake-like with rough, scaly skin. Layers of scales made up the outer part. However, in ratio, the head was much larger than a normal snake's body. It was large and almost human-like, with red, flickering eyes, and sharp facial features. There was no hair or human skin, but eyes, nostrils, very small ears, and a large mouth. It had the most horrible face, so evil, so scary. It opened its mouth and out came a long, forked tongue that flicked at me, like a snake before it strikes. As the tongue retracted, the creature made a horrible hissing sound that I read as a threat to my life.

Instantly, I moved from a feeling of joy unspeakable to intense fear. It was as though panic took over, and I was not sure what to do. Then, again it submerged, and I believed it was coming toward me. In a flash, it surfaced, just ten feet in front of me.

This time, our eyes locked. I could see nothing but evil in its eyes. I was convinced it was going to kill and eat me. My fear now turned to intense panic, and my mind worked furiously. How could I stop this thing? What could I do to get out of this?

About that time, it dove down under the water, with me in its sights. I knew I had to do something, so I dove under the water to try and fight it off, knowing it would not be much of a fight, but I had to try something. Remember, under the water, I could breath and even speak, because this was not normal water.

I could see it coming closer and closer to me, and I prepared myself for a fight to the death. As it came within two feet of me, horror gripped my soul, but then something made it turn and begin to move around me instead of attacking me. As it moved around me, I thought to myself that I should do something to keep it from circling around and making a second pass, so I reached out with both hands and tried to grab the body of the creature, but it slipped though my hands like butter. I gripped with all my might, and nothing happened. I could not hold it at all. It just continued slipping through my hands....

Then I awoke. I was shaking and dripping with sweat. I rose up and sat on the bed, looking at the clock. It was 4:00 A.M.. I was very disturbed and upset. I knew God was trying to tell me something, but what? What was the message for me?

I got up and made my way downstairs to pray. I had to pursue an answer. I needed to know what this message was, so I began to pray two things. First, what was this dream revealing to me? In other words, what was the interpretation? Second, how should I apply it in my life? Needless to say, I prayed like I had never prayed before. Breaking before the Lord in a humility that can only come with a realization that I can do nothing and that only God can provide the answer.

After about an hour in prayer, God gave me the interpretation. He put in my spirit that the lake, all of the lush foliage, and the swimming were representative of His goodness, peace, and joy that comes with walking in and obeying His will. The creature represented Satan and his evil schemes, and Satan was seeking to destroy me and my work for Him. Then great news came with this statement: The Lord said, "Satan will come close, but He cannot have you."

Wow! What a relief to hear these words. Satan desired to attack and destroy me, but God would be my protector. Praise God! It was such a relief to be able to rest in this. I thought the main part was over, so I began to express to my Lord the joy of this revelation and the thankfulness in my heart for His protection. However, I was not ready for His next statement to me. He said, "There will be a problem on the flight today, but I want you on it."

What? Could You please repeat that? A problem? What kind of problem? My mind raced with all sorts of questions—none of them expressed my great faith. I was more trying to figure out how I could get out of this flight. My company had already booked it, and in a few hours I was to be on board. However, as I prayed God kept telling me the same thing. "I want you on this flight."

During all this commotion downstairs, Vonette heard me praying, and got up to see why I was so intense in prayer. I shared the dream and the interpretation. She was thankful to God for revealing that He would protect us, and that His hand would be upon us; however, when I told her about the problem with the flight, and that God wanted me on it, she became very disturbed.

She began telling me that I should just change the flight and not get on it. I let her move through the same thoughts, concerns, and emotions that I had just struggled with. It was approaching 6:00 A.M. now, and I had to be ready to leave for the airport soon if I was to make the flight. I invited her to pray with me about this, and we did.

After that prayer, she looked intently at me and said, "Are you sure God is telling you to be on it?"

I replied, "I am sure."

She then said what we both were feeling. She spoke what our lives were about, "Then you must be on the flight, and we must trust God for what will happen."

I, too, knew this was the only answer we could come to if we were going to be obedient to our God. We prayed again, submitting the day into the hands of our Lord. There were many tears that morning, because we were not sure what the result of this obedience would bring, just that we must obey. I traveled out to the airport that day in a sort of a deep trance of wondering.

It was a very overcast day with intermittent showers. The sky was almost black with cloud coverage. It was like darkness was surrounding me. I boarded the plane and nervously settled into the seat, making sure my seatbelt was tightly fastened. I knew that oftentimes if a problem is going to happen on a flight, it occurs during take-off or landing, so as we prepared to take off, my heart was about to jump through my chest. My hands gripped the armrest so tightly that my knuckles turned white.

The pilot pushed the throttle forward, and the airplane moved faster and faster down the runway, and in a few minutes we were in the air. It was bumpy at first because of weather, but we were in the air and just fine. I breathed a sigh of relief at that point, thinking we were good until landing, but as we moved through the clouds, it was quite a bumpy ride. In fact, at times people were struggling to stand or walk through the cabin.

As the flight progressed, it was as though we could not get out of the turbulence. In fact, it seemed to grow worse. After a little while the captain came over the intercom, telling everyone to sit down and make sure they had their seatbelts fastened. The flight attendants were trying to serve when out of nowhere, there was a bright flash, and a very loud sound rang though the cabin. It sounded like an explosion. The impact was so strong that it threw the flight attendants into the laps of the people seated next to them.

Like an elevator falling out of control, the plane fell for what seemed to be hundreds of feet. Everyone was screaming, and emotional chaos broke out. Immediately, the nose of the airplane began to press forward into a dive angle that told us we were headed down. Not straight down, like a nose down crash, but at such a degree we were not sure what to think.

Flight attendants tried to calm our emotions. I began to pray, asking God to show up and save us. The plane continued its descent and turned sharply to our left. People were losing control. They wanted to know what was going on.

After what seemed to be forever, the captain finally came over the intercom and communicated that they believed we had been struck by lightning. We would be landing right away. There was no question in my mind that Satan had struck, I was the target, and that it was still to be determined what the result would be.

It was quite a bumpy descent, but we were finally ready to land. The pilot did a great job and landed the plane without further incident. I exited the plane and giving praise to my God. I felt I had passed the test. I had not shrunk from it, and God brought me though it untouched, just like the dream had said. Satan had come close, but he could not have me, and that was exactly what had happened.

We were delayed about four hours while the grounds crew checked out the airplane. We then boarded the very same plane again, and the pilot told us that the lightning had come close and almost hit us, but that they could not find any marks at all on the plane and that we were good to fly on to our destination.

I sat in the plane rejoicing in my great God. He was my protector, and my deliverer. He was the only One I would trust in.

Unfortunately, this delay made me very late arriving at my destination and checking into my hotel. By the time I could get to a phone, Vonette thought for sure that something terrible had happened. I called her as soon as I could, and we both rejoiced in our Lord.

Second, Satan is not happy with a heart that is sold out to God, and he tries to counterattack. It was only about a year and a half into the ministry with the singles that Satan raised his ugly head. We were so naïve to the schemes of the evil one.

One of the singles went to the leadership of our church and told them that I was leading our singles in a "charismatic" direction, and that our Friday night prayer times was wrong and improper because it revealed dirty details of singles' lives.

One Sunday, after church, I was called into the pastor's office. He began to speak to me about some of these things. The truth was, I was blown away. I shared with him that only the most honorable things of God were going on, and we had no intentions of doing anything that would in any way harm our singles' lives.

About that time, the one who was so against us came in at the pastor's cue. This person began to compare me to a cancer growing in the singles' ministry. I could not believe my ears. I was a cancer? Why would anyone say this? On top of this, my pastor did not take up for me or in any way defend my character or who I was.

I sat there stunned and hurt. The person continued for a few more minutes. I could not listen to his words. I interrupted and told them that I must leave—I could not sit though this kind of discussion. I would need time to think and pray over what had been said.

I stepped outside and cried out to God, saying, "What do You want from me? I am giving You my all, and this is what I receive in return? I just do not understand."

I went home, and my wife, noticing my countenance and body language, immediately asked what had happened. I shared all this with her, and it upset her. She proclaimed we would just quit. We would not be their teacher anymore. To be honest, I too, had some of these same feelings; however, I was trying to consider what God would want.

About that time, our pastor knocked on the door. He apologized about what had happened, and it did help some, but something inside me would not let go of some of this single's statements. In fact, I felt that God must be moving us on and told the pastor that. The pastor quickly told me that the couple's class was in need of a teacher, and he would love for us to take it if we would consider it. I told him I would pray about it and let him know in a few days.

By the next weekend, I was teaching a couples' class, and it began a life-long commitment to teaching couples about God and His ways.

Years passed and God continued to use us in couple's ministry. We saw a class grow from eight to eighty-five. It was a large, but loving class of adults, caring and serving with such a desire to please God. This was our heart as well—to please God and know Him more, willing to give of ourselves so that others would grow in Him.

Our family had grown. We now had two children, Benjamin and Samuel, and one on the way. My wife had been struggling with her pregnancies. In fact, she was almost emotionally unstable. I would talk with her over the phone and everything would be just lovely, yet by the time I could make the fifteen-minute drive home, she would be a basket case, unable to handle even the simplest of tasks.

Many times, I would rise up and tell her how God wanted her to behave. I would quote Scripture over and over again, and tell her to by faith just trust God and she would be OK. Yet, no matter how much I pointed my finger at her and accused her of not being in the Word enough, or not praying enough, or simply not having enough faith, things did not get any better. In fact, they seemed to grow worse.

This caused a great strain on our relationship. We just did not understand what was going on. It was also devastating to our spiritual growth. I continued in ministry, but she was unable to participate. This was not the way we had approached our ministry in the past. It felt wrong. It felt different. We were apart a great deal. I was at work much of the time and then off to do the ministry in the evenings, and our relationship suffered.

In the summer of 1992, we had reached an all-time low. Something had to change. I was still blaming her for her lack of faith, and I gave her an ultimatum—change or else. Now, I didn't have any kind of "or else" in mind; it just sounded good at the time. About this same time, my company needed me to go to a conference in Gulf Shores, Alabama. Vonette insisted that she come. I was not sure how this would be good, but I agreed. I would be flying, and she would need to drive, because we did not have the money to fly her.

After I had been there a couple days, she and Benjamin arrived (Vonette had dropped Samuel off at her sister's house). I was staying right on the beach, so it was a great place for them to hang out while I was at the conference. We would meet up each day toward the late afternoon and have some fun time together on the beach.

On the last day of the conference, I finished early and met them on the beach around noon. Ben was playing in the sand, and Vonette and I were talking about our relational problems and the difficulties she was having with her emotions. I had been thinking about this and believed I had another word from the Lord for her.

I decided to give her a lecture and using the beach sand as a white board to draw out the lesson so it would be very clear. The lesson was one that Bob had taught us about our body, soul, and spirit man. We were made up of all three, and if Jesus Christ was on the throne of our spirit man, then He influenced everything else, even our souls, which were made up of mind, will, and, that's right, emotions.

I carefully drew all this in the sand using three circles to represent each component. The first and largest circle represented the body. The second circle, within the first, represented the soul. I divided the soul circle into three components and labeled them mind, will, and emotion. Then, I drew the third circle within the second one, and labeled it spirit. Within this third circle, I also drew a throne, or a chair that represented a throne.

I began to ask her who was on the throne of her heart, or spirit? Was it Jesus Christ, or self? I shared with her that if Christ is on the throne of our spirit man, then when trials and circumstances come into our lives, we will be able to repel them with the power of God. If we are on the throne of our lives, then the circumstances can control who we are. *Great teaching*, I thought.

About that moment, God spoke into my heart. He said, "This is exactly the way I want you to look at your marriage. You and Vonette are one, and if you are one, and I am on the throne, then *together* you will be able to repel the circumstances and stand firm in Me." What? I had something to do here? I was responsible for helping her stand firm? I needed to stand with her? I had not been doing that. I had been criticizing her and accusing her of being weak.

The Lord shut my mouth that day and would not let me speak anymore for days. I was so overcome by His message that I could not speak. I gathered my things and left for home on the plane. I arrived that evening and went to bed, and Vonette began her two day journey home.

I lay in bed repenting of my selfish heart. I cried out to the Lord to forgive me for treating her this way. I remained in bed for all of the next day because God had His hand on me, and I could not get up. That evening He released me, and I arose and pulled out a book that we had about having a godly marriage. I read the entire book by the time my wife returned home.

Upon her arrival, I sat down with her and committed my life and my help to her in whatever way that she needed it. I was a different man and a different husband. I finally understood that we were to be one in this battle. I was now ready to roll up my sleeves and help her through the trenches of this difficult time.

Needless to say, our marriage has never been the same. God used this time to grow us together in our relationship. To this day, we remain committed to stand and fight together through the difficulties and circumstances that come our way, knowing that this is the way our God intends it to be. Two are so much stronger than one, and when the third One, our Lord Jesus Christ is added, it forms a bond that cannot be broken.

A little later, we *together* sought help for her from a doctor, and it turned out that with medication this hormone imbalance and post partum depression was treatable. The doctors worked with her and helped a tremendous amount, but God used this most difficult time to shape our marriage into the godly union He desired—a marriage that is one in Him.

Chapter 10

THE CALL TO PREACH

> When he had seen the vision, immediately we sought to go into Macedonia, concluding that God had called us to preach the gospel to them.
>
> —Acts 16:10

It was Thanksgiving, 1992, a wonderful time of year. Thanksgiving always brings the reminder of the event that changed our lives forever, some eleven years prior. Our family had now grown to include three rambunctious, but precious boys.

Vonette was busy about getting our family ready to travel back home for Thanksgiving. We planned to stop off at my mother's home on the way to spend some Thanksgiving time with her, my brothers, and my sister. Then we would travel on to Vonette's home town and spend the rest of our week, including Thanksgiving Day and through the weekend, with her mother and extended family.

This was a trip much like we had done many times, nothing really out of the ordinary, but something we enjoyed and looked forward to. The idea of seeing all our family and friends and sharing God's blessing with everyone was something we enjoyed. It is what we did on Thanksgiving.

All went according to plan for the trip including stopping to see my mother and family and pressing on to Vonette's home. On this trip, we were planning to attend Vonette's old home church on Sunday. This had a special place in our hearts, because it was the church where we first professed Jesus Christ as Savior and Lord. It also was the church where so many people came to our rescue while we were going though our difficult time before and during our jail stay. So, to worship with friends for the first time since our release and, to rejoice with them about what God had done in our lives, and to fellowship together would be like icing on the cake for this holiday time away. It would be sweet.

The Thanksgiving time went very well, first at my mom's home, reminiscing about childhood fun and exciting adventures. Then at Vonette's, we enjoyed a wonderful two-way pass of information, bringing each other up-to-date. Friends and family shared what was new and going on in each others' lives. Then we all said our goodbyes and settled in until Sunday.

Sunday came, and we loaded up the car with children, clothes, diaper bags, and leftover sacks of chips, canned drinks, and a partially uneaten pumpkin pie. We were headed to church about thirty minutes away and immediately after would leave for home, a seven-hour journey.

We were excited but a little nervous about visiting our old church. We both understood, but never talked about, what kinds of emotions we would feel. They would be unpredictable, but they would come—as surely as the morning breaks each day. Without saying a word to each other, we knew, let the emotions come…we'd be okay.

We arrived at church for the Sunday morning Bible study classes, and I was asked if I would share what God was doing in our lives. Of course, I always take any opportunity to tell people what my great God has done for me. They ran and called several classes together so many could hear.

It was a good time. People's lives were touched, and the Holy Spirit was powerfully present. I was thankful for this, and the people voiced their appreciation for my sharing. Time was soon up, and now it was time to move into the worship service.

I was busy fellowshipping and was almost late for the starting hymn but quickly sat down beside my wonderful wife. We settled in among the three hundred or so people for what I hoped to be a time spent with Jesus Christ through the power of His Spirit.

The service started in an old, traditional style by singing hymns and, of course, the collection of offerings. We were currently members of a contemporary church, so it was good to sing the old hymns, and I worshiped the Lord through them. I enjoyed the deep reflection and strong theology that each hymn seems to sing out. Little did I know what was about to happen.

The pastor stood and began the message. After about five minutes into his message, I was getting frustrated. He was not making sense to me. He seemed to be unprepared. It didn't appear to be going anywhere, and there was no power from the Most High.

I was not very happy. I wanted more that day. I wanted a hot word from God straight from the throne room right into my heart. One that would challenge me, motivate me, move me off of dead center, one that I could shout out, "Amen!" about. You know, a real barn burner.

I began to tune the pastor out and chew on the Lord's ear. I was asking Him, *What is going on here? These people need to hear the pure Word of God, something that will move them and help them grow in You.* I was really getting into it and complaining in my spirit.

When I finally stopped to take a breath, the Lord spoke to me. Now, God had spoken to me many times in a variety of ways but to this point in my walk with Christ He had spoken audibly only a very few times. However, God spoke audibly into my mind and heart, and this is what He said, *"Doyl, this is what I want you to do. I want you to preach the Word of God to people just like these."*

I was staggered! Needless to say, I did not hear another word the pastor said. I sat in a stunned state of mind that I could not shake. My mind exploded with reasons that this command was ridiculous. I could never preach the Word like a preacher or pastor. I couldn't because I was an ex-con. Didn't God know I had been to jail? I couldn't because I had no training. I couldn't because I was too old to start that kind of journey. I couldn't because I had a wife and three children. I couldn't because I had a wonderful job and career. Then I stopped. I literally told my mind to be quiet. I took a deep breath.

Right then, my wife slipped her hand over and touch my leg, looking at me and quietly asking me if I was all right. I nodded in a reassuring way that everything was fine, but inside, I was pretty rattled. First of all, rattled that the divine God would consider me worthy to even speak to me, to call my name. My God called my name. This was overwhelming to my soul.

But I was also rattled that He would tell me to do something that was such a privileged position in the kingdom. I tried to focus, but I could not. All I could think was how could someone like me do anything like this for the Lord? Well, about that time, "Just as I Am" began to play. The sermon was over. The call had come. Now, what would I do with it? That was the question.

At the conclusion of the service, Vonette began to say her goodbyes to her friends and family that was there. I tried to participate, but I just could not get into it. I finally leaned over to Vonette's ear and whispered, "I need to talk with you, now." She looked at me strangely but understood that something had taken place. So she quickly finished up, and we moved outside into the parking lot.

I couldn't hold it in anymore, so there, in the parking of this home church, I told Vonette what had happened. She was both excited and guarded. Almost immediately, she voiced that we needed to stay and have lunch with some of our dear Christian friends as well as her cousin. I agreed. She went off and found them, and they agreed to meet with us.

We met at the local truck stop for their buffet lunch, and I was able to share the call of God on my life. They rejoiced and were not surprised. They had thought that something like this might happen. It was God speaking a confirmation through these wonderful saints. This just reassured me of my conviction and helped me solidify my faith. I was so thankful for them and how God used them at this time. Over the years, God has used this couple in mighty ways to support, encourage, and stimulate obedience to God's will in my life.

When we arrived at home, Vonette and I shared a nervous excitement. I believed that God had called me to preach, and yet I did not know what this would mean for our future. This was a healthy tension for us, because it drove us to our knees often. We talked over the next steps and settled on the obvious one—to share this great news with our pastor.

Our pastor was a kind man but very driven in the vision that God had put into his heart. He had led a traditional worship style church into the main stream of contemporary worship. He knew and voiced that God was taking our church into greatness.

I arranged an appointment and met with him to share my news. He gave a warm embrace, but I sensed a guarded choice of support words for me. I just read it that he needed time to hear from God to confirm my calling.

He told me two things. One included the idea of licensing me for the ministry. He explained that this was not a full ordination; however, it would allow me to preach, teach, marry people, and bury people. The full ordination could not happen for an extended period of time. He even gave no commitment that our church would ordain me. I didn't fully understand, nor was I concerned about it much at the time. He also asked me to let him know when I was ready with a prepared sermon, so we could schedule a Wednesday night for me to preach. I was excited to hear this. This is what God had called me to do.

The last thing I mentioned, before his secretary buzzed in to tell him his next appointment was waiting, was that I wondered if our church had help for someone like me, providing a pathway, a set of steps or guidance, that could transition me from my secular job into the full-time call to preach the gospel.

He told me that was a great idea but that our church did not have anything like that put together. I then asked if he would be willing to meet with me on occasion to help me understand what this call was all about. He gave some guarded response; I couldn't even grasp if it was a yes—maybe it was a, not now, or a no.

Again his secretary buzzed, and this time he picked up the phone and assured her we were finished. Our meeting ended, and I left unsure of how to feel. I was excited about the licensing, I think, excited about the opportunity to preach, but very puzzled about the lack of real, genuine interest. Maybe he just needed time to seek God, so I would not let this meeting distract me or dampen my spirit. I would move on, trusting the God who had called me.

Over the next few weeks, I worked very hard on my first sermon. I even remember the title, "The Message of the Cross." After getting it in the best shape I could, with no experience at all in preaching, I placed the call. The secretary arranged a Wednesday night for me to preach the Word.

I was so nervous that night. My emotions were running like wild horses chased by a bobcat. I did not know what I was doing. I did not have any mentor to model or even confirm that I was on track. One thing that especially was missing—there was not even a phone call from my pastor. Well, I thought he just wanted to see what I was made of.

It was a large worship center, able to hold some fifteen hundred people, in which we had about eight hundred on a good Sunday morning. A typical Wednesday night crowd would draw some ten to fifteen percent of our Sunday morning attendance. Of course, our friends and the special people in our lives were in addition to the regulars.

The service began and progressed along as normal. Then the time came for me to preach. As I stood up, my eyes scanned the crowd (well, to be honest, not much of a crowd), looking for my pastor, hoping he would be there to support this young, newly-called preacher, but he was nowhere to be found. Shaking in my boots, I opened my Bible, pulled out my notes, and did the best I could.

Afterwards, so many encouraged me, but I could tell by their faces I had a lot of work to do to become the preacher God had called me to be. However, I had my first one under my belt, and I was eager to do it again. I was ready to preach every Wednesday night. That would be great, and it would help to prepare me for what God had called me to do.

The next day, I set an appointment with my pastor to find out what he thought about this idea and what should be my next steps. We set a meeting for about two weeks out. In that meeting, he dropped a bombshell into my heart. He told me that it was not the vision of our church to "give up" the pulpit to men like me (newly called to preach). He said the Wednesday night was just a one-time event to prove that God truly had called me.

The truth was, he really did not have time to spend with me, and he advised me not to give up my "day job." I was so hurt and humiliated, and I felt abandoned. As I was driving home, emotion flowed like a river. I almost could not drive. I became upset with God. I began to complain, asking God why He would call me and then give me a pastor who was not even able to support me. I just went on and on.

Finally, when I ran out of things to list, God spoke clearly and powerfully. He said, "Man did not call you, I called you. I will teach you, train you, and test you. Put your eyes on Me." Well, needless to say, I stopped my complaining and began asking for forgiveness for how quickly I had turned to man for solutions to something that God had called me to do. I promised myself that I would not let this happen again (big words that it would take years for God to develop in my heart.)

Equipped with my new surge of faith and fully dependent on God, I began to share with my friends and family that I would be willing to preach anywhere at any time. I just did not know anything else to do given that I had no direction from God to go to seminary.

Time passed, and I was able to preach several times in the next year at our home church in Louisiana, at my mother's church, and at a few of our friends' churches. However, to be honest, things just were not moving fast enough to suit me. A year had passed since I received the call from God to preach, and I had only preached a half dozen times, including the one time at my church.

I was getting very frustrated with the whole situation. God had called me to preach, but it just was not happening. What did my wife and family think? What did my friends think about this seeming delay? Did they read it as a delay, or were they thinking I was a fool and had not been called by God? Again, I boldly told God that I couldn't do this. If He wanted me to preach the Word, He would need to make it happen. I was through trying to do anything on my own. I think that God must have said something like, "Finally."

Several months passed, and I had settled into the idea that maybe God was trying to see if I was willing to say yes. That was possible; maybe He was just testing me to see if I would be obedient to the call. Yes, that must be it. Why else would nothing be happening, certainly not enough in the visible world to suit me? But soon all this would change.

It was a bright, sunshiny, spring day, not a cloud in the sky. The temperature was perfect, not too cold and not too hot. I was up early that morning, spending my time with our Lord, when the phone rang. On the other end was the pastor of a local church.

I had met him about two months earlier at a birthday party for a mutual friend. I had only just briefly met him, and we had conversed in very casual greetings, and then he had to leave. He was a nice young pastor, and he seemed to have a deep desire to follow God in his ministry.

Our phone conversation began with the usual greetings, then he said he needed to tell me something. He began by saying, "Every time I pray about a revival for our church, your name comes to my mind. Would you consider preaching a revival for our people?"

I laughed. I told him I had never done that before. In fact, I had only preached about seven or eight messages to this point in my preaching career. He responded, "I know, it sounds ridiculous, but I believe that God is putting your name in my mind. Would you please pray about it?"

I told him I would consider it and pray about it. For the next two weeks, I fasted and prayed, asking God what to do. How could I preach a series of messages when I had not ever done anything close to this?

Well, explanation did not come, but what did come was a simple directive from the Lord, "Trust Me." I knew He was telling me to move forward, and He would reveal what I needed when I needed it.

After two weeks of fasting and praying, I called the pastor to let him know I would preach his revival under these conditions: First, I had no idea as to timing for this revival, and we must wait on the Lord for the date. Second, I had no idea what the sermon topics would cover. I would go to the Lord, and He would tell me. Third, we must fast and pray at least once per week for God's direction and anointing. Fourth, we must meet every Saturday morning to pray together, seeking God's will and answers. To my shock and surprise, the pastor said yes. I could hardly believe it. He agreed.

Time passed, and we fasted and prayed. We met together, seeking God's direction and guidance. And we became as close as brothers in Christ. God was faithful. He began to pour into my Spirit the sermons and direction for this revival, and finally, he gave us the date. It would be held in the latter part of October, a fall revival. That sounded good and exciting—to finally know a date after so much prayer.

I was working full time in a very demanding job, teaching a Bible study class at church, discipling several individuals—this sure added to my to-do list! I had to accomplish much each and every day. But, spiritually, I was pumped. God had spoken. I would obey. He would bless. That was my philosophy.

The date finally came for the revival, and I was nervous. Not nervous in the usual sense but nervous to see how God was going to move. How would He fill my expectations of His Spirit moving and changing lives?

God did move in an awesome way during the revival. The church was packed each night. The people were on the edge of their seats, full of expectation for what God would have for them each night.

The Spirit of God moved like I had never seen before by just preaching the Word. People were so moved that each night the altar would be filled with thirty or so people weeping, confessing their sins, and wanting to walk in obedience with the Lord. Fifteen people came to know Jesus Christ as Savior and Lord.

Each night, ten or so would confess their sins before the congregation. This was something I had never experienced before. Needless to say, God moved mightily. I was so excited and humbled that God would, or could, use me in this way; however, this was just one of the great ways God moved during that time.

The second way He moved was just as incredible if not more so. He changed me. God had called me two years before to preach the Word (almost two years to the month), but it was during this revival time that God anointed me to preach. This is very significant. Something happened to me during the time that is almost unexplainable.

It was as though during this process God forced me into a Spirit walk that could only be supported by Him. He demanded that I seek Him, follow Him, hunger for Him, obey Him, hear from Him, walk with Him, know Him, believe in Him, and to taste and know that the Lord was good.

It was like God has some kind of anointing jar in heaven that He uses when we are ready for His commissioning in our lives. At the beginning of this revival, God raised up the anointing oil in heaven. He poured it forth into my life, and it ran down, consuming my mind, heart, and soul. The anointing oil of the most high God became the flow of the Spirit of God within my life, and I was changed forever.

I went back to my Bible study class, telling them I was not the same. I must preach the Word. It was in me, and it must come out. If that is what they were looking for, then this would be the right class for them. If not, they needed to go somewhere else and attend some other class. They cheered me on and encouraged me to move with the Spirit. I am very thankful for saints who support and encourage those of us who have the special call to preach the Word.

At this point in my life, I had to preach the Word even if it required me to step out to the street corner to do it. You see, there was now a fire burning inside me that I could not put out, nor did I want to extinguish it. I just wanted to tell anyone who would listen about the truths of God. This fire continues to be my passion to this very day. May God receive all the glory, amen.

THE CALL TO PLANT

Blessed are the pure in heart, for they shall see God.
—Matthew 5:8

Now, loaded with this new fire from the most high God, I began a new season in my journey with the Lord. There was still almost no interaction with the leadership of my church, and I just kept on doing the things I believed to be God's will for my life. I taught the Bible class each week, discipled several people on a weekly basis, hosted special prayer times at our house, engaged others in Bible studies in homes, and supported our church and its ministries. In fact, I started a children's program in our church and became a major player in the evangelism thrust of the church.

Our pastor had been going through a transformation from the idea of a contemporary church to a new concept called, seeker-sensitive church. He had traveled to a conference and caught the vision for this new approach for reaching people. He had been transitioning our church for a year or so, and there were still a lot of questions about what all this meant.

Anyway, the Lord began to stir in my heart. He was speaking through my restless spirit and longing for the meat of the Word; however, I could not and would not take a step unless God gave us direction. I believed He would, so we waited on the Lord, to hear His voice and know what He wanted for us.

I had to make a business trip to Tampa, Florida for the company where I worked. We had some computer software problems, and I was sent down to look into them and to try my best to fix them.

I was staying in a hotel that was located on the St. Pete Beach in Saint Petersburg, Florida, just across the way from Tampa. Late one night, I arrived back at the hotel after having a light dinner. I changed into my running shorts, shirt, and shoes. It was about 9:30 P.M., and I decided to relieve some stress by running on the beach.

It was a nice night, and the stars were against the backdrop of a very black sky over the ocean. I ran and walked for some thirty to forty-five minutes before retuning to my hotel room.

After my return, I sat down thinking I would do some work before I went to bed. Suddenly, the Spirit of God fell upon me. I opened my laptop and began to document what God was speaking to me.

God was pouring into me, like a pitcher of water onto a new plant, a detailed vision for a church. Beginning with the worship service, an approach to the preaching of the Word, Bible studies, children's programs, discipleship, prayer, mentorship, etc. I wrote and wrote until the wee hours of the morning. When I closed my laptop, He had developed an awesome vision for somebody's church. Now, I wasn't sure whose church but certainly someone's church that God would reveal.

When I returned home, I couldn't wait to call up the pastor of the church where I had preached the revival. I invited him over to my house, thinking that this vision was for him and his church. God had used me mightily during the revival, and I just thought this was an extension to what God had been doing. Boy, was I shocked at his response to this idea.

The pastor came by my house at the appointed time, all ears. I believe he was thinking I was going to ask him to allow me to partner with his church. Meaning, I would come alongside him and support his ministry and vision, adding support to his infrastructure.

I shared the vision God had given me, moving through each sheet of notes, sharing with excitement and anticipation, believing it must be for his church. So many of the items in it were areas where his church was struggling and needed help. He had voiced this during our prayer and fasting time before the revival.

He sat silently, waiting until I finished the complete concept. I straightened the paper as I finished and asked him, "Well, what do you think?" His response was not what I expected at all.

He replied, "Don't you think you should join our church before you talk with me about such things?" I was shocked! Join his church? What did this have to do with anything? What could this possibly have to do with a God-given vision for a church? He went on to say, "Vision must come from the pastor!" I was staggered. I slumped back in my chair and replied, "OK. This must not be for you."

You see, I thought I knew it was for him, so why was he rejecting it? I must have missed the mark here. It must not be for him, and God must still need to reveal where this belonged. I was absolutely convinced it was a vision from God, so now it was a matter of finding for whom it had been given. I began a quest to see who that might be.

I again set up a meeting with my pastor. After sharing the vision God had given me, he too, rejected it, saying, "We have a vision here, and it's not within our vision as a church to plant other churches." Well, another no.

I left that meeting wondering, no, crying out loud toward the heavens, *If not these two, then who Lord? Why would You give me a vision for a church that no one wants? Who is it for, God? Tell me!* I finished my outburst in a demanding tone. I am so thankful for the understanding and patience our God demonstrates toward us, His impatient children.

Right after I finished this outburst, the Lord spoke to me in that rare audible voice, almost in a whisper, "*Start a church.*"

I was on my way home from the meeting with my pastor and almost ran off the road. I turned down a street and came to a compete stop on the side of the road. I slipped the gearshift into park, took a deep breath, and said out loud, "What did you say?"

Again, the same voice came. "*Start a church.*"

I responded with all the great spiritual phrases, "What? Who am I to start a church? I have never done that before. I do not know how to start a church. You must be kidding, right?" But nothing came—not another word—just the echo of that still small voice, the voice I knew so well by then, speaking a simple message to start a church. I tried to compose myself. I made the rest of the trip home without incident.

When I arrived home, Vonette was there working with the kids and doing her normal things around the house. I walked in and sat down, trying to decide whether to hold this information to myself or share it with Vonette. I knew so much was unanswered: the why, where, how, when, with whom. And what about my work, my family, my home? So many unanswered questions. I just wondered how all would play out in Vonette's heart. Could she take the stress of not knowing? Could she walk with me through the unknown? What would be the outcome? When would we know the answers to all these questions?

About that time, Vonette punched me and said, "What is wrong with you? I have asked you the same question three times, and you act as if you haven't heard anything I said. What is going on? How did your meeting go?"

I could not keep this from her. In fact, I needed her to walk with me and beside me through what could be the most challenging time of our lives to date. I told her I needed to talk with her in our private prayer area right away, and she said OK. She got the kids settled down into cleaning their rooms while we retreated to our prayer area.

She broke the silence with the question, "Doyl, what is going on?"

Well, I struggled to find the right way to share. Finally, I just let it go and told her that God had spoken to me to start a church.

With her voice elevated, she said, "How do you know it was God saying that? You do not know how to do something like this. When does He want you to do this? Are you sure?" She came with the flood of questions that I knew she would have because I had all the same ones.

To be honest, we would need to seek God for answers to each and every one of them, but for now, we needed to address a different issue. It was the issue of saying yes or no to God.

Since we began our walk in Christ, we had never knowingly said no to God. Whatever He wanted us to do, we did to the best of our ability. I, for one, was not ready to start saying no, nor was Vonette.

This was a very important, big decision for us. We felt the weight of it on our souls. It was like there was a spiritual battle beginning to be waged in and around our minds and wills. Our minds were being flooded with doubts (which is common anytime God calls) and our souls were gripped with fear. We were not fearful of failure, but the fear of not knowing for sure this was really God calling us to move forward.

So I proposed a plan. We would take a plan from Gideon out of Scripture where he too was trying to make sure he was about to do the will of God. Two times he used the fleece to determine the will of the Lord. God is not afraid of a pure-hearted test from His children to determine his will. We both agreed. We would pray about two things that only God could do and lay them before His feet. If He did them, then it was His will for sure. We would embrace the divine direction to start a church.

We fasted and prayed for a week, seeking fleeces that would be appropriate. This was new ground for us, and we wanted not to offend God but rather to please our Lord through seeking His will intently.

The Lord spoke to me specifically about the fleeces. He not only wanted us to do this, but He spoke to me about what they should be. I shared this with Vonette, and she agreed. If God answered these two fleeces in a positive way, we would obey His known, revealed word.

Together, we laid them before His throne and trusted Him to bring them about. (You might be wondering what they were; however, the Spirit will not allow me to share this most intimate interaction with my Lord. Clearly, there were some things Paul was unable to talk about, and the fleeces are something I cannot reveal, restrained by the Spirit.)

It was Christmas time, and we had a wonderful celebration of the birth of our Lord. We shared with family and friends how much our Lord meant to us. Christmas came and went. January and February came and went without incident, without answers. Then, on March 1, the Lord answered the first fleece. I remember racing in to tell Vonette that we had a positive response to the first fleece. She was subdued, almost guarded. I asked, "Aren't you excited?"

She answered, "The second one is much harder; we will see."

It wasn't that she was not interested, but she had learned from days past that we needed to guard our emotions and wait until we knew for sure. I took her lead in this area and tried not to get too caught up in the excitement of the possibility. Within two weeks, the dam broke. God had answered the second fleece positively.

I called Vonette into our prayer area to talk with her, this time with holy fear of the Lord. Excitement was present, but the fear of the Lord was overwhelming. I told Vonette that we had the answer to our second fleece. It was positive, and I believed God had confirmed the call to start a church.

At first, she made excuses, thinking of all the reasons we should not do this. In the natural, she was right, but this was not something in the natural but of the Spirit.

I finally interrupted her and said, "I believe God has confirmed that He wants us to start a church, and if we are going to live an obedient life to the Lord, then we must take this step of faith! To obey God is the only way I can live for Him." There was silence in the room for what seemed to be a long time.

Vonette raised her head, looked right into my eyes, and said, "Then start a church is what we will do. Count me in."

Praise God, we both had come to the same conclusion. We must follow hard after God in order to be obedient to His will for our lives.

I told her, "Don't worry, given that I do not know what I am doing, it probably will not last over a few months anyway." I realize this was not a man full of faith, but God would overlook this weakness in my faith and create something that would last.

The time had come to set an appointment with my pastor to share this great news of how God had spoken and moved in such a powerful way to confirm His will for my life.

I still did not know the timetable, but I was ready to yield to the leadership of my church for that. I set the appointment and looked forward to sharing this news with my pastor. The meeting started with our normal warm greeting and concern for each others' lives.

Then, I introduced all that God had been doing since the last time we had talked. The pastor seemed to embrace it all. He was somewhat encouraging, talking about when God called him and how challenging this step would be.

I agreed and expressed my desire for our church to bless and support this step of faith with anyone who would like to help. I told him I would love for our church to define the steps and timetable of how things should move forward. He told me he would take this request before the elders. At some point, he said he would like to bless us and send us off in front of the body to show his blessings.

I left this meeting greatly encouraged. Within a week, his secretary called to inform me of a special elders' meeting to talk about me and my request.

As I walked into the meeting, the air was cold. I felt a shiver move down my spine. The men present would hardly look at me. I felt as though I had done something wrong. I proceeded to share the vision God had given me, and His call to start a church, finishing with the request for their support and help.

Without any discussion, without any prayer, and without any hesitation, one of the elders began to tell me how wrong I was. They would not support me or help me in any way.

Before this time, I was one of the most respected Bible teachers in the church. As far as they were concerned, I was hearing from God each week, teaching the Word, and making a difference in people's lives. Needless to say, I was stunned. The same elder then proceeded to ask me, "Now, what are you going to do?"

I almost couldn't collect my thoughts. I simply said, "Well, since biblically, you were supposed to be the ones to support this direction, God will need to raise someone else up to support us. And He will."

They had already decided all this before I arrived, and they had it worked out as to who would say what. Then the pastor told me I needed to leave the church immediately, take anyone who was with me, and not talk to anyone else in the church. I simply agreed, knowing that God would accomplish His will. This was not the way I had envisioned our church reacting to this great news, but it was reality.

So in April 1994 with seven families and three singles, we began Pure Heart Fellowship Church the very next Sunday in my home. It was a meager beginning, a very humble beginning, and we had no clue about how to proceed.

I would spend all day on Saturday preparing music on tapes so we might worship on Sunday. Our music department consisted of a Sony boom box and a pre-recorded tape. We would move the couches against the walls, bring in folding chairs, set them up, and just have church.

I lead a children's Bible study at 9:30 A.M., we would start worship at 10:30, and then I would preach for a couple hours. I would say that I have come a long way from this, thank the Lord. However, we moved forward with pure hearts and a desire to see God move in others and in us.

Chapter 12

MOVING US FORWARD

I press on toward the goal for the prize of the upward call of God in Christ Jesus.

—Philippians 3:14

The challenge to keep my full-time job and pastor a church was becoming increasingly difficult. I would work so hard all week and then spend most of the weekend studying, preparing, or engaged in church activities. There were times when I didn't think I could keep it up, but our church could not afford for me to step out and become a full-time pastor.

There was one particular time that my job required I travel to the Northeast to work on a proposal for the government. I would be gone for nine straight weeks, working fifteen-hour days. I didn't know how I would be able to preach and be in the Northeast at the same time.

Normally, when you were on a proposal assignment of this duration, the company would fly you home two times at the most. This was their policy, but not when you are a servant of the most high God!

During this assignment, something would always come up, and I would need to fly back on Friday afternoon or Saturday morning each of the nine weeks. Each time, my boss requested I fly home on the weekend and back on Sunday night or Monday morning, to which I would readily agree.

During those nine weeks, God always brought me home in time to hold our church services, and then I would be off to the airport to return to complete my assigned task with my company. God is a great God that works out everything we need to accomplish His will.

In January 1995, PHF moved from our home into a 600-square-foot storefront building. When we moved into the space and set up the folding chairs, we didn't even fill it half way up. We were so small. What could we do for the Lord? But God blessed this step of faith. People began to visit our little church, one of them asking why we met in the "break room."

We grew in size and maturity. Our people began to step up and take on roles they had never before done in a church setting. We began an outreach program, ministering to newcomers in our city. We began a children's program that was second to none.

God kept adding to our numbers slowly, but in time we grew out of that space and needed more. So, we rented another 600 square feet, then another 500, then more and more…until we had taken up over half the available building.

Now, it was time to consider implementing two things. One, a fulltime pastor. I would need to resign from my very lucrative position with a prominent defense contractor, making a wonderful salary. God had shown such favor to me at this job. They had blessed me with double promotions and large raises; however, my life belonged to the Lord. Whatever He wanted, I had to do. It was now time to seriously consider stepping out into full-time ministry even though it meant taking an over fifty percent pay cut to do it.

It became obvious that eventually this was going to be part of the sacrifice required to follow His will.

The second thing was the purchase of land for the church. This needed to become a priority. We were running out of space, and we would need a building soon. In order to continue to grow, we needed to move on this right away, and we did.

To lead a congregation in the purchase of land is no easy task. There were so many thoughts, ideas, and even opposition to the land-purchase strategy. God had spoken to me about the purchase of land and the construction of a new building; however, there was one in our elder group who began to put forth the idea of just continuing to rent space and make do.

Our by-laws required one hundred percent consensus in order to move forward. This man's thought process was one that seemed to be owned only by him. It took some time to move through this as an elder group. It seemed that once he had an idea it was very difficult to move him from his thought process. At one point during our meetings while discussing this topic, I challenged him to go find us anything that could meet our needs as a church in our area.

Within a few weeks, he was willing to open up to the idea that we must purchase land and build because within our bedroom community we really had no rentable space that could service our needs.

Praise God! Immediately, I did two things. One, I introduced the idea of a land fund to our body. To this point, we had not been raising money at all for land, and it was time to do this. I read about how the building committees of the 1700's would prepare for building a church. Their first act as a committee would be to plant a grove of oak trees, providing the needed lumber for the future building. This would be the oak beams for their large cathedral. In a hundred years or so, when they needed the large oak beams, the trees would be there. What vision, what planning, what a thought process. So, we began by donating $250 to purchase our symbolic oak trees.

Next, I created a land search team. I purposely excluded myself from the land search team, trying not to unduly influence them in their search. I believed I would have plenty of influence later. I launched them out to search our area for suitable land possibilities and to give us a report on those possibilities. In the meantime, I was fasting and praying that God would reveal to me the site that was to become the perfect location for Pure Heart Fellowship Church.

One day, when I was out in our community, I passed by a piece of land on the main thoroughfare in our city. The Lord spoke to my heart and told me to turn into this piece of property. It was ten acres of prime real estate in the middle of the city. All the new city growth was just north, and most of the older part of town was just south of this location.

As I turned off the motor and stepped out of my car, my heart and mind began to race. Would this be the place? Was God speaking? This sure would cost an arm and a leg. How would I know for sure? How would I go about looking at it? So many questions, but I had never attempted to purchase commercial real estate before in my life. These were questions that must be answered in God's timing and within the context of a church not just a passionate pastor. I would lead in the Spirit of God, trusting Him to reveal truth and location and His perfect will for PHF. I walked over the property and prayed.

I returned home from this divine moment excited, but guarded. I shared it with no one. Over the course of the next couple weeks, I drove by this piece of property and stopped each day just to seek God. I prayed and asked Him to reveal if this was the place for us.

It was on a Friday, around noon. I went by to pray over the site. I had been fasting that day, seeking His will. As I walked and prayed over it, the Lord spoke to me, and said, "This is yours." I dropped to my knees and began to lift up praise to my God and Lord for revealing His will. It was such a powerful moment—simple as I write about it, but profound at the time. My God had communicated to me the exact location to purchase that someday would house a church in the name of our living, most high God.

Now, I had another question. How would I communicate this to our land team? Would I just tell them, this is where it will be built, go purchase it? Or would I be patient and prove the will God? How would I handle this? Well, God spoke to me again. He did not want me to share it with the church just yet, but to wait and watch what He would do. This was very difficult. I had what I believed to be the location of our church and yet could not speak it to anyone in our church. In the mean time, our land search team was busy about finding a location for us to purchase, and they were working hard.

After just a few months had passed, they had found about thirty-five different possibilities meeting their criteria. This criteria included: the land must be within our ministry area; it must be a minimum of eight acres of land; and must be located on a main artery (highway) of our city.

There were so many possibilities, each having its good and bad points. Now, the real work began for them. Sorting through each prospect and trying to seek God's will tested their faith, their resolve, and their skills. After about six months of work, this team had narrowed their original land prospects down to five very good possibilities. They then called a meeting and decided it was time to walk over each location and pray because they did not have any idea which would be the right one for us.

They invited me on these prayer walks. It was a powerful time together as we broke in prayer over all that God had brought us through and felt the excitement and anticipation of where He was leading us. We had some very powerful times in prayer.

After a month of listening for God to speak, they decided to call another meeting and invited me to come. In the meeting, the team leader communicated to me that they were just not able to reach a decision. They had worked so hard but were not able to discern God's will as to which piece of property was the right one. I sat and listened. When I saw their frustration and earnest desire to find the right location—knowing God had already revealed the location to me—my heart pounded with excitement and humility.

And guess what? The location that God had revealed to me was one of the five locations they were still wondering about. Isn't this just like our God? Who are we to thwart the will of the most high God? Who among us can stop His perfect will from moving forward? Can we in ignorance re-direct His purpose? I think not. I know, we cannot.

I remember leaning in and looking over all of the drawings and notes spread over the table where we were meeting. The air was thick with wonder and puzzlement. There was a question mark on each man's face. I just simply said, "I believe I know where God wants us to purchase land." There was silence. A hush came over the meeting. You could've heard a pin drop.

Finally, the team leader said quietly, "Pastor, share your thought with us." So, I pulled out the drawing that contained the different land options. I leaned in and pointed to the aerial photo-map revealing the location that God had shown me much earlier.

I said, with great authority, "This is where God desires PHF to locate."

After a short period of silence, the leader spoke and said that this seemed good to him. We then moved around the table, asking each man what he thought. They each, one-by-one, confirmed that it seemed good to him.

At the conclusion of this agreement, my heart was about to explode. Not with pride, but at the power of my God—the God who can move hearts. He revealed His will some six months earlier then moved the minds and hearts of men to become unified to move His church forward.

I asked them to pray to see if it seemed good to the Holy Spirit. We had one of the most tender, yet powerful, prayer times. At the end, we all agreed it was good to the Holy Spirit. We would go forward, share this decision with the church body right away, and begin to pursue the land purchase.

The following weekend after our land decision, Brother Bob and Pinky traveled over for a visit. I took him to see the location we were going to pursue. We began to pray over the property, and two things happened.

First, Bob received confirmation from the Lord that this was the site for PHF. It was so reassuring to have my spiritual mentor confirm where God had led me to build His church.

Second, God gave me a vision. A wonderful vision of how He would bless this place. In the vision, I saw people all over the ten acres. Not buildings, but people, families. Lives were being changed and transformed by the power of God. This was a tremendous vision. It motivated me to move and caused my faith to rise up with a newfound power to believe in great and wonderful things from our God.

We left the site with a sense that all would work out fine, and soon we would own the property. Someday in the not too distant future there would be a beautiful building on this site named Pure Heart Fellowship Church.

Bob left in time to make his church service back home, and I moved on to minister that Sunday. I shared with our people about the decision, and everyone was so excited. We all knew this would require sacrifice, but first we wanted to rejoice in knowing where God wanted us to locate.

I must admit, we had a few naysayers among us, expressing how there would be no way we could afford ten acres in the city. There would be no way that we as a church could purchase the land, much less build a building. I tried not to let this heart of doubt influence my mind and brushed it off with hope, and a heart of faith. It was time now for action. It was time to inquire about our piece of property. I would do this on Monday.

I arose early on Monday, anticipating a glorious day in the Lord. Today was the day He would explode His will on the scene like a blast of dynamite. Today, I would see Him split the sea of real estate and allow us to walk through on dry ground. Today would be a day that would go down in the history books of PHF as a day of the Lord's hand moving on our behalf. Today would be the day I had been waiting on for years—a great day in the Lord.

I completed my quiet time and moved on to accomplish a few small items that were on my to-do list, waiting until the real estate office opened. I placed the call at the nine-o'clock hour, hoping to find the agent in the office, but I had to leave a message.

I tried so hard to go through the day as though it was no big deal, but my heart was full of excitement, and it would not allow it. It was about two in the afternoon when the call was returned. There was a nice man on the other end who asked me which property I was interested in. I told him which property we were interested in purchasing. I also mentioned that we'd like to know the listing price and asked who we could talk to about it. Immediately, he asked me to hold on. I agreed. After what seemed to be an hour, he returned with information that I was not prepared for.

He said, "Mr. Tully, I am sorry to inform you that a contract was placed on that piece of property yesterday morning, and it is in a ninety-day verification stage." He continued, "Provided all goes well, it will close within ninety days."

I was devastated. Inside, I cried out in agonizing pain. *What? Wait a minute. You don't understand. God has told me that this is our property. We must purchase it. It must go to us, not to someone else.* Finally, I regained my composure enough to thank him and ended the call.

I was hardly able to breathe. How could this be happening? God had spoken. God had confirmed. God was God. My flesh seemed to rise up. To be honest, I got angry with this. How would this make me look to our people? Our people would begin to doubt my leadership and the direction of our church. This would be very challenging for me as a leader. Full of self-pity, I was worried about me. I immediately called Vonette and shared with her the very confusing news. She too did not understand what God seemed to be saying. We both had to agree by faith that God has His ways, and they are not man's ways. He had a different approach in mind for how we would get this property.

After praying and getting my flesh out of the way, the Lord told me to put a contract on this property. I told Him, "They already have a contract on it." It did not matter. All I kept getting was that I was supposed to put a contract on this property. So I finally said, "OK, I'll see what I can do."

So, I called up the real-estate man again and asked him if it was possible to put a contract on this property even though someone else had one in place. He shared that we could place a "back-up contract" on the property if the seller was interested. The back-up contract would go into effect if the first contract fell through in any way. Only then would we have opportunity to purchase the land. I quickly said, "OK, let's pursue this idea with the seller. Please contact him and see if he is willing to move forward with a back-up contract." And we did.

In fact, the sellers not only agreed to allow a back-up contract, but I entered into negotiations with them and finally settled on an agreed price of $385,000, which was some $65,000 less than the agreed price on the first contract. Can you believe this? I really do not think the seller or the real-estate person thought this contact would ever be an option.

However, the price tag, even though a much better price than the first contract, was still way out of our reach as a small, upcoming church. We would need a miracle from our God to purchase this land because we did not even have a down payment, much less $385,000. Anyway, we were able to get agreement from the owner. Now it was time to wait and see what God would do.

I had called Bob and shared this with him. He returned over the weekend to support and pray me through it. We went to the land site to pray. As we walked the land and prayed, again the Lord spoke to Bob. Bob shared that if the owner would allow us to plant an oak tree on the property, it would be a sign that this property would be ours. Wow! What a communication. I did not even know who the owner was, much less how to approach him with a request to plant an oak tree on his property.

I shared this with our elders after Bob left. There was skepticism. There was resistance. There was a thought that I was trying to make this happen and not allowing God to move us forward. I refused to believe that this land was not ours; however, doubt did creep in at times.

I began to pursue locating the owner of the land. I needed to get his permission to plant this oak tree. I asked the real estate person, but he could not give me the information due to professional reasons. I understood, but that did not stop me from pursuing who this owner was. I checked with the land office and found out the person on the title did not even live in our city, nor could I find any known address.

I was almost at a stand still. I prayed one day, telling God that I needed this to be fulfilled to increase my faith. I needed His touch and confirmation. Like Abraham had multiple revelations about the same promise, I needed another confirmation, desperately.

About that time, the Lord spoke and told me to ask the renters. I remembered that there was a rent house on the land. They had to pay rent to someone! So, I stopped by their home and asked them who owned the rental house. They quickly shared the name and exactly where he lived—only about three blocks away from our land site. He lived right in the neighborhood.

That afternoon, I went unannounced to his home. I knocked on the door. He answered, and I identified myself as the pastor of PHF and told him I would like to talk with him for just a minute. He told me he could not talk with me about the purchase and that the real estate agent took care of all of that type of business.

I told him that I was not there to talk about the sale but to just ask him a question about the property. He reluctantly invited me in, and we moved to the back porch. As we sat on his back patio, I began to share about our church and our people. I was really trying to work up the courage to ask a question.

Finally, I just said, "I have a question I would like to ask you. Would you allow our church to plant an oak tree on your property?"

He looked at me strangely and said, "What an unusual request." He was silent for what seemed to me an eternity. Finally, he broke his silence with these words. He said, "Do you see all of these trees in our back yard?"

I replied, "I do."

He continued, "Over the years, my family has planted all these, but there are only two types here. One is the pecan tree and the other is the mighty oak tree. We love oak trees. Sure, you can plant an oak tree on my property."

All of heaven seemed to explode in my heart with joy and excitement at that moment. I know he had to think I was crazy, but this was all I needed to hear. I told him our elders would be by to plant the tree this next week, and then I thanked him and left. My heart soared for I knew this land would be ours someway, somehow, someday—and there was no doubt about it.

After the elders and I planted the oak tree, I moved to engage our entire congregation to believe God for this land. On the next Sunday after church, we all met at the land site to pray over it. I had all the people stretch out over the land from one property line to the other.

Then I instructed them to take a step and stop and speak, "I proclaim this land to be ours in the name of Jesus Christ for the purposes of God." Then, we would take another step and repeat this proclamation. It was a glorious sight to see. Some forty families stretched out over the property, doing something they had never done before, believing God for something they could not see happening in man's eyes. Yet they were applying all the faith they could to believe God for the impossible. It was a great day for our people and a great day for our church.

On day eighty-nine of the ninety-day evaluation phase for the first contract, I received a call from the real estate agent. He informed me that the first contract had fallen through for some reason, and our contract was activated. Therefore, we had sixty days to purchase the land.

Sixty days to find a bank to borrow the $385,000 and close the loan. A bank that could look at us and believe we could do this. Where would I go? What bank would loan us this kind of money? Who would be able to see our potential and not our current meager beginning? Only sixty days to accomplish so much. We needed the absolute favor of God.

I began a quest to find any loan institution that would listen to my pitch. My pitch included that I was not yet a full-time pastor as of this time, but making plans to become full-time; we were very small (maybe 100 people by now); we were just able to meet our financial needs each month; and we had no collateral—but I had a great deal of faith!

Armed with the belief that God was with me and He was in this purchase, I put together the best financials possible from the beginning of our church to this time in 1996, showing that our finances and membership had increased each year.

Within a week, I had knocked on about half-a-dozen bankers' doors, submitting this proposal for the ten acres. However, by the end of the first thirty days, I had received all negative responses to my requests for loans. I was getting so concerned. Only thirty-days left before our contract would run out, and we would lose this opportunity.

During this same time period, while discussing the loan possibilities with each banker, I found out that we would need to come up with a significant down payment if we were to get any loan. In fact, most bankers were talking about $50K-$60K.

We had nothing—maybe about two thousand dollars in a reserve. I took this to the people, asking them to seek God about how they could respond to such a need. I also asked them to give generously as a step of faith, believing God was going to give us this land. We must pool all the resources God had blessed us with to see what we might be able to do.

Our people began to ask God what to do, and they began to give. We were within three weeks of our deadline and still no bank loan with only about $15K raised for the down payment. Time was running out. I was running out of options.

One day, as I was driving home, I passed by a very small, one branch bank that somehow I had overlooked. I had currently approached all the large, visible banks in our area. Also, all the banks our people personally used had been approached.

This one was under the radar. It was so small that I really had not noticed the location. The Lord told me to go in and talk with them. So I made a u-turn, and went by to set an appointment.

I was able to get in that afternoon to talk with the one and only loan officer. I shared our vision as a church and as a business proposition, trying my best to convince him we were worth the risk. We would come through. At the end of my familiar spiel, I finally allowed him to speak, and he was ready to say a few words. The words that flowed from his mouth told me instantly I had finally come to the place God would use for us.

He said, "Mr. Tully, I am a Christian. The president of this bank is a Christian. We love to help churches get on their feet. We would be glad to look at the possibility of completing your loan."

This was music to my ears. It was as though all of heaven exploded in song. I had to catch my breath and hold my emotions in check. I shared with him that we only had about three weeks before our contract was up and that we needed to move quickly.

He gave me instructions, a request for additional data required from us, and some formats that needed to be followed for the loan process. I went off and completed all this within a few days. We were before the loan committee within two weeks and had an approval for the loan in hand.

The only problem we faced now was a $60K down payment requirement. This was challenging. To be honest, this was somewhat overwhelming. We had one week to complete the fund-raising, and to this point, we had only managed to raise some $30K. I went back to our body and shared this need with them. The land purchase came down to this bottom line: We needed an additional $30K within a week to receive the loan. All the work, faith, and effort came down to this financial need. I called our church to a week of fasting and prayer. We would seek God for His provision, and we would trust Him for the result.

The next Sunday was an unbelievable Sunday. During that week, one of our members was blessed by an unexpected sale that gave them the resources to give an additional $10K. Another member had stock that surged forward to make a fifty percent increase and allowed them to give it to God. Another member sold a home, which generated a large equity sum that enabled them to give abundantly.

By the time we came to church on Sunday, we were just $3K short of our need. We took up a special offering, which then provided some $5K, putting us over the top and on our way! On Monday, we signed the papers and closed the land deal. Praise be to our God for His abundant provision. Some ten plus years later, this same $385,000 ten acres is now worth over $1million. This is just a wonderful testimony of how God provides and expands our resources, so that we can accomplish His will.

Up to this point, I had been working full-time for a defense contractor and performing full-time duties as a pastor of a small, but growing church. We were now settling into the routine of having church each Sunday, reaching people, paying for land, and looking toward the future of a new building someday. By 1998, about four years into the start-up of our church, it became obvious that I could no longer continue in a secular job and maintain the demanding schedule of a full-time pastor.

The time had now come to step out by faith and only focus on the church. However, this would mean a salary for the pastor, which to this point had been zero. I had chosen to allow all our giving to be turned back into the growth and needs of our body.

My salary up to this point was just a way to make enough to live and tithe on, so that our church would be able to move forward. I was one of the largest givers at this time, so stepping out to become the full-time pastor with a salary would be a major hit to our church finances. It would require our people to step up to make up the difference and to provide for the needs of my family. And they did.

Our people, armed with a heart of giving and sacrifice, were full of desire for a full-time pastor with a salary. We moved forward with this approach, and God blessed our faith. By 1998, I had become the full-time senior pastor of our church without the distraction of a secular job. My family was very excited about this move; however, later our faith as a family would be greatly tested. Vonette and I seemed to know in our hearts, without a word being said, that now we must trust in Him completely for our provision.

Armed with this new freedom, I pressed us forward toward growth, both spiritually and numerically, along with our vision to build.

It was during Vision Night, January 1999, that I communicated that we must move forward with a new building. We had been paying on our land, but it was not helping us reach people in the current state. I felt we must move forward to locate on this site as a church. That night I introduced our new building fund and asked our people to begin to support it.

Some of the first real grumbling took place after that night. Some of our people began to complain and make comments about how we as a church weren't positioned to go and build a building. We did not have the resources or numbers to support something like this. Actually, some people were excited about the potential of constructing a building to reach more people for our Lord—and that is exactly what we should be about. So our fund increased ever so slightly.

In June of 1999, I was praying about our new building and almost complaining to the Lord about the lack of support from our people. We had only raised about $5K in six months. This would not build anything. How would I lead our people to build if they would not catch the vision for it? I was really chewing on the Lord's ear about this, and God spoke to me so clearly in a voice that He only has, "You have no plans." Yes, that is exactly what He told me. How could I expect God to bless us with a building if I had no plans for one?

The real issue was that I had not had the faith to move forward with plans up to this moment. I was waiting on the provision rather than moving forward expecting it to be in place just when we needed it.

This is how God works so many times. Hold up the name of the Lord, step into the water, and watch the waters part. Well, this was all I needed to light a fire under my faith. The next Sunday, I shared with our elders and body that I wanted to move forward with hiring an architect—a firm that could help us put together a plan for our new church building.

Wow! What I got in return was not what I expected. I expected joy, excitement, and a readiness to move forward by faith. What I got was resistance, arguments, and grumbling—and they were right with their logic.

We only had about $5,500 available to do anything. What could we get for this little amount? What would we do after spending this? We would have nothing. What if we had a difficult giving month? We might need this money. All these observations were true; however, I believed God had spoken. I pushed hard for them to allow me to move forward with this plan. The elders agreed. The body complied. I moved with a shaken faith, but hopeful heart that God would reveal Himself in this step.

I located a firm that would be glad to use up our $5,500 with just a master site plan for the ten acres and the first cut at a floor plan for our new building. I created a team to give our input to the architect. About six months later, they yielded a floor plan for our new 13,152 square foot building—and a completely depleted building fund.

It was around December fifteenth when we completed the drawing. I shared this drawing with our body the next Sunday. Some were excited to finally see what our new building floor plan might look like. There was an excited buzz that morning; however, the naysayers were out in full force. They criticized the effort and went so far as to say that this was not God's will. We did not have the money to do this.

I began to pray as we moved into the Christmas season, praying in a statement of obedience and accomplishment to God. I said, "Lord, I have a plan now. I now wait upon You. Reveal who You are to all." God was silent. Nothing ... The Christmas of 1999 came and went without a word. It was a good Christmas and a meaningful one for our church. Vonette and I agreed that we were now in a "wait on the Lord" posture.

We had just moved into the lull between Christmas and New Year's when I received a phone call from a person from another state. This was someone who had been supportive of our ministry all along the way, mostly in personal helps and in small needs within our church. We loved him very much and had often wished he and his wife lived within the area of our church, but that was not to be. They were hundreds of miles away and where God wanted them to be. We prayed for them often, and they for us.

A few days before New Year's, I got a phone call from this dear friend. His name was Paul Meeks. The Lord had used him in a very powerful way early in my struggle with the arrest. Paul and his wife, Melonie, are Christians and Melonie is Vonette's double first cousin (you figure it out.).

When we had hit rock bottom from our circumstances, God used Paul and Melonie to encourage, support, and help us move through our difficulties. There was a time when no one else would hire me because of my potential trial outcome; however, Paul came forward, put his arm around us, and provided a job for me within his business. This was a job he created knowing I may not have time to really understand his business or make much of a difference, but he did it out of a loving, merciful, and giving heart.

Many times since then, they have helped us, mentored us, and come forward just in time. We give God great praise for friends, partners in ministry, and Christian brothers and sisters who will put action to their faith and be used by God to advance His kingdom. We love them deeply.

Over the phone, Paul took a few minutes to catch up with what was happening in our ministry and family. I shared with him where I thought God had us as a family and church. Then he asked me a question.

He said, "Can I make a donation to your church building fund and still get it on this year's "statement." I told him if he placed it in the mail today, it should arrive in time and would be recorded in this year.

Now, he had given in the past, and this was not an unusual request. I just answered it in a way that you would any question asked of you about something like this. We finished our conversation with our usual goodbyes and blessed one another in the Lord.

I went on about my preparations for our January 2000 Vision Night. This was a regular event in our church. Each January, I would share what I believed to be the direction of our body over the coming year and beyond. In this way, I tried to keep our people connected to the vision. Vision Night was set for about January 15th, and I was busy preparing for it.

I never will forget New Year's Eve, December 31, 1999. It was a good day, bright, sunshiny, and unusually warm for a New Year's Eve Day. I was a little warm wearing the sweater I had on. I had retrieved the mail on the way home and carried it in with me. Once I arrived, I settled into opening the mail in an everyday, normal mode. I recognized a small envelope from my friend—something a small card might arrive in. I laid it aside. I would look at it last not for any particular reason just that was my thought at the time.

After going through the junk mail and few bills that surfaced out of the stack, I then turned to his envelope. About that time, my wife had called out my name to ask me a question, so I picked the envelope up and walked upstairs to see what she wanted.

I was opening the envelope as I made my way upstairs and by the time I arrived into the bedroom where she was, I had it opened. What was inside was a personal check that was folded in half. I looked for a card or letter or even a small note, but I found nothing. Vonette continued asking her question as I took the check out and unfolded it.

From this point on, I did not hear another word from Vonette—not because she was not talking—I was just so taken up with what I saw. I opened the check to find it made out to our church in the amount of $200,000! And in the memo line was the simple phrase, "For the Vision."

I lost my breath. I know my face must have gone white because the next sound I heard was Vonette saying, "What is wrong?"

Well, nothing was wrong, and everything was right! I began to scream out that our friends had sent a check for $200,000. I jumped for joy, screamed with excitement, and shouted praise to God. Vonette wanted to see, and she too joined me in celebration. Here we were, two people in a small town in Texas, relatively unknown to man, convicted felons, changed by God, moved to obey Him in every way we knew how, now seeing the awesome, powerful hand of God move in this way.

It was just overwhelming, and we both broke before our God. We gave him praise and glory and lifted up His name for what seemed to be hours. There are no words to express the incredible presence of our Lord at that moment in our lives. God is an awesome God. Our friends will not know this side of heaven how greatly they were used to move the kingdom work ahead. God's plans are not man's plans. God's ways are not man's ways.

I managed to keep this a secret, although I do not know how, until our church Vision Night. During that night, I shared with our people that we were going to build this year and that we would be moving soon.

Well, it was received with some lack of response, like some were just putting up with a pastor having delusional thoughts and dreams. I felt like Moses for just a moment there as I told the people to stand back and see the glory of the Lord. I then shared about the $200,000 donation that the Lord had given us for the vision. There was a gasp. There was silence. An eerie kind of silence that spoke volumes about the mind of man.

They were trying to process all this. They were trying to make sense of it, but they couldn't. Finally, after what seemed to be five minutes, someone was so overtaken that they began to applaud. More and more joined in until all were standing before the Lord with loud applause and tears streaming down faces. I called our music team up, and we sang songs of celebration and praise, and I danced before the Lord in the presence of all, proclaiming His great and continued provision.

Now, armed with this $200,000, I had a whole new confidence in our next steps as a church, and new respect from our body. They had watched God bless and honor my faith, and they were willing to listen more to the direction that God would be taking us through my leadership. This was very key. A congregation must be willing to follow in order for leadership to be most effective. Now, our church was willing to follow.

I now began the process to complete our plans for the building and secure the funding for its construction. This would be a task I did not fully understand, and it would take every skill, talent, and ounce of faith I possessed in order to complete it.

I really had no idea what I was stepping into. I just knew this was the will of God for us and that I would obey His direction, so I pressed forward. I met with the architect and moved the plans forward. This was easy compared to the financial part and finding the builder.

Now that we were packing a $200,000 bank roll, our bank was more than ready to help us with a building loan, and our architect was well on his way to developing the complete set of plans. We searched high and low to find a builder we could trust to give us straight answers and good numbers to work with.

The bank now wanted a complete, believable budget for the new building. Our first half dozen builder costs came in at $1.5M and up. As I brought this to our bank, they would not go for it. It was too much debt for us as a church to incur. And on top of this, we needed to roll our land cost into this loan, which would run the number up another $330,000.

After months of searching, receiving bids, and meeting with builders, we settled in with someone who gave us numbers the bank would finally agree to. These numbers were more than reasonable and to us seemed realistic. However, later we would find out that this contractor was just telling us what we wanted to hear and manipulating the numbers to win our business.

Almost one year passed before we could finalize the plans and the budget and secure the building loan of some $1M to began the building process. In the end, we would have our building and ten acres of land owing some $1.3M. This seemed like a lot for a small church, but we continued to grow. In fact, we had to move to two services to handle our crowds. God continued to bless all our efforts.

The first three months of construction were a disaster. The builder was unable to get anything done. He and his crew were just not experienced enough to handle this sized project even though they had given us documentation that seemed to show otherwise. We had to put them on a constant watch and review, which did not seem to be appreciated from their point of view. They were draining our funds with practically nothing to show for it.

To top it all off, the bank had given us only one year to complete the building project, so time was very precious. In three months, only a little dirt work on the site had been completed. Things had to change.

By month four it became painfully obvious that we would need to fire this contactor and try to replace him. I prayed much during this time, asking God to intervene and bail us out of this mess, but nothing.

I remember the day I fired this contractor some five months into the project. After I let him go, I walked over the abandoned job site. All he had completed was a slab and some of the concrete parking lot poured. It was a long way from a 13,152 square foot building.

Emotionally, I was down, and a depression was trying to set into my soul. I fought it off, but it was so strong. I finally looked up and cried out, "You must do something and fast. This is your church. Help me!"

We were able to find a new construction manager and began to get a few things moving. However, he too was not a person with the experience to accomplish the job. We'd get the materials to the job site, but no one there was able to get the building going.

This led me to a decision that I made without understanding how challenging it would become. I decided to take over the project and become the general contractor. I had no experience in this, but I had a vested interest. This was the church of the living God, and I would do everything in my power to make it work.

We were at the end of six months into the project when I went to work. I would work twelve to fifteen hour days, six days a week, preaching on Sundays, and then returning to handle the building. God raised up a man from our congregation named Carl who became my right hand man. Without him, we would not have the building we have today.

Day after day, week after week, we worked. In fact, I worked so hard that my family suffered greatly. At times Vonette would plead for time with me, not for herself, but for the boys. I would squeeze in an hour or two, and that was just all I could do. She was being both mom and dad to the boys. She kept telling me our fifteen-year-old son was acting strange at times, but could not put her finger on why. We just hoped it was that adolescent time of discovering "who he was." My life seemed like a run-away roller coaster. I'm grateful to the Lord that He had kept His hand on my family during that time, even though I couldn't.

We had hired some framers to come in and erect the outside walls and ceiling beams. They had almost all the outside walls up, including the front forty foot high walls. However, they had not completely tied them together, breaking for the weekend and planning to complete it early the next week.

Our church had a workday on the weekend to put up some exterior sheathing. I was up eighteen feet on an exterior wall. We were having very strong wind gusts; so much so that it would almost blow us off the scaffolding as we tried to attach the sheathing. About that time, a twisting type of wind hit the front of our building, and the whole front swayed and moved and finally collapsed into a metal heap on the ground.

Two massive laminate beams were fully exposed because the front of the building was gone. We ran away from the building, thinking it was all about to collapse. Praise God, it didn't; however, the entire front was gone—piled up in a twisted heap of metal.

I walked to the other side of the building, away from everyone else, and began to weep. I cried out to God saying, "What are You doing? Here I am doing all I know to do to build this church, and You are allowing it to be destroyed. Why? You have got to help me."

After a silence, and when I had calmed down some, the Lord spoke to me. He said, "Do you see that twisted pile of metal?"

I replied, "Of course I see it."

He continued, "Just like these walls are twisted and bent and broken into a pile, there are people whose lives are the same way in this community. I want you to minister to them, and I am going to restore them unto Me. Now, re-build the walls."

I cannot share with you all that God did in my heart during that very private, yet public, object lesson. There is no doubt He allowed this to happen just so I would clearly understand the direction of my ministry to come. To this day, the twisted and hurting come to us for healing and restoration in the name of Jesus Christ.

We moved forward, and God did show up. Our people did so much of the work themselves: all the electrical, HVAC, painting, much of the drywall and insulation, landscaping, irrigation, and much more. We saved as much as $400K in the process. It was a good thing we did because even with all of these savings we still spent $950K to construct the building.

To the bank, it looked as though we came in right on budget, but the truth was, we invested so much to make this building happen. God went before us and enabled us with whatever we were willing to do to accomplish His perfect plan and will.

I thank God for Carl, for the way he stood with me and allowed God to use him in such a big way. PHF exists today because of our partnership as we labored together for His kingdom. I also thank God for a loving, patient wife who put up with so much so that our church could be built. Without her steadfast faith and loving support PHF would not exist.

We completed the building and moved into it on a beautiful day in July, 2001. What a celebration! Paul and Melonie and Bob and Pinky drove over from Louisiana. Vonette's mother and sisters all made their way to the celebration. What a glorious time for us as a family and as a church family. Each church member placed a stone of remembrance as a testimony to our great God. This pile of rocks, located just in the front of the church, serves to remind us of God's mighty provision for our building. As a church, we remain alive and working on behalf of our Lord Jesus Christ to this day. To God be the glory, amen!

Chapter 13

LIFE LESSONS

O God, You are my God; I shall seek You earnestly; My soul thirsts for You, my flesh yearns for You, In a dry and weary land where there is no water. Thus I have seen You in the sanctuary, To see Your power and Your glory. Because Your lovingkindness is better than life, My lips will praise You.

—Psalm 63:1-3

My life continues to be dedicated to serving God in obedience to His call. A call that is not completed nor fulfilled. I believe the best God has for us always lies ahead. He always wants to move us forward in His plan, purpose, and will. He wants what is best for us. He desires to make us into something we cannot, or will not, imagine—for His is the infinite, and we are the finite. He is the divine and we are the created. We are the fallen, and He is the perfect. We are the blemished, and He is the unblemished.

I am more than convinced that if we will but yield our souls, hearts, and minds to Him, He will shape, mold, and develop us into something that has great purpose and impact in His kingdom.

He is no respecter of persons. God will use anybody. Yes, that is right, even you.

I would like to leave you with the three truths I have tried to communicate in this book.

FIRST, THE HEART OF MAN IS ARROGANT AND WICKED

Left to our own thoughts and ideas, man is so perverse. The best of man—anything he can conceive—falls short of being anything good and righteous. We just cannot hit the mark of righteousness.

I was guilty of allowing my thoughts and life to move down a path of self-righteousness. Understand that arrogance is a pathway that will lead you step by step into the most wicked ways. It will lead you to such a point that you will find yourself justifying your every wrong action.

Many want to think they are "good people" and will remain good in-and-of themselves without needing the presence of God. This is only a lie from the evil one. The sad thing is that man continues to buy into this in ways that lead to his great destruction. Lives are ruined day-in and day-out by this arrogance. Every man, woman, and child must come to grips with this truth. I am wicked in thought, ways, and life. Righteousness is not possible within me alone.

SECOND, THE PROFOUND GRACE OF GOD IS FOUND AT THE END OF A SIMPLE REALIZATION OF NEED

This great news is so wonderful. God has not left us at the end of the road of wickedness. He has made a way for us if we will but realize our profound need.

At this point in my life, I came to this realization: I had a desperate need for God. That's right, a *desperate* need for God. I did not have all the answers. In fact, I did not have any answers. I just realized my condition and need. In doing this, God flooded my mind with one simple thought. "Jesus Christ died so that you can have life. Receive this openly and honestly, and you shall live. You will have life like you have never experienced before. A life with purpose, hope, and a future."

I wanted that kind of life. I needed that kind of life. I simply asked Him to come and help me to be what He wanted me to be, and He did. As simple as that sounds, that is all I did. But, it was not all He did, nor is it all over yet.

God has so much more in store for anyone who will simply and completely give his or her heart to Him. Will you give Him your whole heart? Will you realize your desperate need for Him? Will you invite Him to take charge of your life? If you will, He will, and you will never be the same.

THIRD, THE IMPOSSIBLE EXISTS FOR THOSE WHOSE HEARTS ARE FIXED ON GOD

Once we have God in us and working on behalf of our lives, *all things become possible.* This is so unlike what the world can offer us. Theirs is one of "work hard and good things will happen." As Christians, we cannot rely on what the world has to offer, neither on how hard we can work, nor on how much we can do. Now—through Christ—there is so much more.

We serve the Divine—all of deity—the Father, the Son, and the Holy Spirit. What is not under His rule? What is not available to His call? What does not move at His will? What cannot be accomplished at the beckoning of His command? What can stand in the way of His desires? What can gain victory over the most high God?

I am convinced there should be no greater mindset for Christians than for us to affirm in every situation, circumstance, challenge, difficulty, storm, struggle, or negative thing that God can and will call the impossible possible for us. He'll reveal who He is in our lives to accomplish His purpose. This is our God. This is the God who rules and reigns on high and in our lives. This is who we serve.

Let me encourage you to live the impossible through the God of possibilities.

To order additional copies of

BROKEN
to
RISE

Have your credit card ready and call:

1-877-421-READ (7323)

or please visit our web site at
www.pleasantword.com

Also available at:
www.amazon.com
and
www.barnesandnoble.com

Printed in the United States
52620LVS00004B/292-390